Lucky to Be™ Lutheran:
The First 101 Reasons Why

Lucky to Be™ Lutheran:
The First 101 Reasons Why

Dennis C. Brewer

First Edition

Copper Cove Publishing

Contents

Contents

Contents

Contents

Statement by the Author

For those not familiar or involved with the Christian faith, please let me explain the inconsistency you may find with the idea of your purchasing this book. If my being a Lutheran Christian and talking or writing about my faith, my religious views, and my personal beliefs offends you in any way, then do not buy or read this book. If this written witness to the Good News of salvation for all is a problem for you, then please just leave this book on the shelf for someone else who would have a mind open enough that might appreciate whatever nuggets of wisdom and inspiration this book may contain. If the idea that there is a God who created all things, that Christ accomplished a redemptive work on the cross at Calvary for you and all mankind, and that you can see evidence of the daily working of the Holy Spirit in our lives and in the world rubs you the wrong way, then this book is certainly not for you. Please find, purchase, and read something else.

On the other hand, if you wish to occasionally be amused as you read, are seeking to become a brand-new Lutheran or Christian, or want to simply get some insights into what it might be like to be and live your life as a Lutheran Christian, then you might find some value from buying and reading this book. Keep in mind that these are my religious views and personal beliefs brought about by a lifetime of attending Sunday services at many Lutheran churches of the Missouri Synod in the United States of America, both the regional district churches and the nationwide/worldwide English District of the Missouri Synod. For the record I have also attended for various reasons during my life a few Roman Catholic, Methodist, Presbyterian, Baptist, Assembly of God, and some of what I would now label as "Brand X" churches. From these experiences I fully understand that Lutherans do not have exclusive rights to call themselves Christian. They do, particularly in this day and age, have a responsibility to see that the Gospel message is preached in truth and purity unadulterated by the evil in the world and by current events or trends in modern-day secular or religious thinking.

For any pastors that might be slumming around in the pages of this book, what I would like to say to you is that this is what you-all have collectively made as a religious understanding and beliefs in the mind of one person from your collective preaching and teaching over many decades. This book is a big part of what was burned into my brain from sitting in the pews of well over 30 Lutheran churches across many states and over a 66-year time span nearly every Sunday. I sat in churches for Sunday worship in both regional district churches and the wider net of the English District. I would guess I have listened to nearly a hundred called and ordained pastors in the LCMS. Some of these thoughts and ideas of mine can also be attributed to my fellow but now nameless churchgoers. Preach the Gospel in the manner you do, and this is what you may be achieving as a system of beliefs in the flocks you preach to, or maybe it's just me. Your output product as a Lutheran pastor is after all creating and maintaining a believer in the true Christian faith and an adherent to Lutheran doctrine; another soul for Christ, another saint on both sides of the curtain of death.

My fellow Lutheran readers, my hope, my wish, my prayer is that you will benefit in some way from reading this book. If you are already a Lutheran of any of the many persuasions of Lutheranism, my hope is that you may be both amused and enlightened a bit and that your faith may be amplified knowing that you are not the only one thinking this way about our shared faith and belief in Christ as Savior. If you agree with some of what I wrote, then there are two of us in that special synod for sure. If you disagree with me, think of it as a good enough reason to start a conversation with your own pastor: most pastors love answering questions and clearing up any misunderstandings you may have about your faith.

For my fellow Christians from other denominations and for those in other faith groups—Catholic, Jewish, or whatever denomination or faith group you may belong to—my hope for you is that you will enjoy the read, learn a few things about our Lutheran idiosyncrasies, and realize that most, yet certainly not all, of the foundations of the Christian faith are the shared bits. Furthermore, my sincere hope is that you will accept that we Lutherans take the tenets and principles of the Bible seriously. Both our history since Martin Luther and the scholarly work done by our seminary professors' study of the early church include information and knowledge that is now a part of Lutheran doctrine and practice as found in the Book of Concord. This combination of historic documents and scholarly work has resulted in our LCMS getting the fundamentals and nuances of the Christian faith exactly correct in what we believe, teach, and confess to the extent that is possible for mere humans to achieve.

To those who have not found or embraced the Christian faith in any way and yet might happen upon these pages, my prayer for you is that you would read this book first with an open mind. Secondly, read while embracing the idea that there might be more value to you from living the life of a Christian over and above a life limited by the repudiation of God's intent for you to be saved. We believe Christ's saving work is offered up for all the world's humans, over all time: *all* includes you.

And a final word to those of you who profess to be Christian, profess to be believers in the existence of God but do not find yourself in a worship service on a weekly, regular, basis because you think you can be one without a church of any kind, know this. The word "church" first of all does not mean a building; it refers to a community of people that share the same beliefs. Setting yourself apart from the church (community of believers) does nothing for you and works to your detriment in every way possible. You are not worshiping a digital God and in addition being alone makes it impossible to be an active participant in the community of believers. Without some divine intervention you will not learn anything new; you will not be well known as a believer here on earth (essentially denying your already weak faith); you will not share in fellowship or in the joys and burdens of being a participating believer. That is like being in a chess club, paying your dues, and never going to a match or a meeting. By not being in a worship service, you unnecessarily deprive yourself of the gifts of communion, a shared peace, renewal of your faith, new knowledge of and insight into the will of God for your life, and the opportunity of supporting one of the methods of spreading the faith and its countless benefits to a needy world.

Disclaimer

This author is not an official, employee, or agent of any one of the Lutheran Church synods or corporations or affiliate organizations. Therefore this book is in no way to be interpreted as an official publication, voice, or opinion of the Lutheran Church–Missouri Synod, nor does it in any way speak for the synod or its corporations, affiliates, pastors, professors, teachers, or lay leaders.

The author is only a lay member of the church body and a member of the universal Christian community of believers. His only role in the Lutheran Church–Missouri Synod is as a church attendee and member of one or more of its earthly congregations.

Realize completely that I have no right to speak for the Missouri Synod Church itself. I do, however, feel free to speak as a *product* of the church's collective efforts to share the Gospel to all in both speech and print. I will in no way diminish that understanding, or apologize for the impact those messages had on me and my religious thinking that I share with you here in this text.

How This Book Came to Be

I have written a number of books on many subjects published by national and international publishing houses that you would recognize, and like most authors, I have a few fiction manuscripts lying about that may never see the light of day or ever be finished. This book came about from a little flash of inspiration just like many of my other books. I suppose inspiration arrived for two reasons. First, I wanted something to write about, something fun to write about, I had been bouncing a few ideas off my commercial publishing agent for other technical books without a lot of enthusiasm on her part to peddle them to a publisher. So, for a day or so, I was mostly out of new ideas.

Then, when leaving for work one day, I thought of how lucky I was, or I am (you pick), counting my blessings really—nice house, two new nice cars, a motor home, one loving wife, a very good job, all the accoutrements needed to be living a decent life, none of which I felt like I particularly deserved. During the day between my commute into work and my commute back home,, and then later that day, I kept counting and recounting my many blessings in the form of "lucky me," and the idea (inspiration) occurred to me: You know, Dennis, you are also very lucky (blessed if you prefer) to be Lutheran. So very, very lucky. There are probably a hundred reasons why I feel lucky to be Lutheran. And these would all be fun to write about.

The second reason: I wanted to write something that at least one other person on the planet besides my ever so supportive and loving wife, Penny, might want to read and enjoy. Writing books has to be about marketing, which almost immediately raises the question; would anyone else like to read that book? I must confess as a writer that I am not much of a reader like everyone thinks or says you should be as a writer. I am very selective about what I am willing to give up my time to read, time that I could spend on writing instead. So, in my limited experience I don't remember coming across any books written from a layperson's perspective about being a "dyed in the wool" Lutheran Christian. There may be a hundred of them out there, so I will apologize now to those who have taken on the work of writing them. I just don't remember ever finding one.

So, for the next few days, perhaps a week to ten days, I wrote down a reason I was "Lucky to Be Lutheran" on my always-present 3" x 5" index cards every time a reason occurred to me. I wrote short one-liners that for the most part described why I feel totally blessed for being brought into the Lutheran Christian faith as a child and sticking with it into and through adulthood. I suppose anyone could and should be feeling just as lucky, thrilled, blessed, and thankful for coming into the faith yesterday, or today, or right now, this minute, this second: The rewards are exactly the same. So, for the rest of this book, I will share with you those thoughts that came to me over those few days, some or all if you are willing to stick it out to the end of the book. Bringing my children up in the Lutheran Christian faith may be the only real, solid gift I have ever given them. Therefore, this book is dedicated to my sons Jason and Justin and all of God's children.

How to Read This Text

Each individual section of the book, all 101 of them (102 if you count the bonus), is an amplification of the first sentence after the number. As you read each numbered reason, preface that first sentence after the number by uttering, for example, after #4: "____ *(am/is) Lucky to Be Lutheran because . . ."* We can respond to the question "Are you saved? . . . Are you born again?" with an unqualified YES. Still using the example from my reason #4, in the blank space you can fill in the pronoun "I," meaning yourself if you are Lutheran already or if you want to become one. If you are not, you can insert my name: "Dennis is Lucky to Be. . . ." If you are from another faith and are contemplating a marriage to someone who is Lutheran, insert your intended's name in the blank space: "Mary *or* Martin is Lucky to Be Lutheran . . ." to get some insight into what your beloved may believe. You get the idea: The book title applies as the beginning phrase of each of the sections' very first part of the sentence. After personalizing each of the reasons, please proceed and read and enjoy the rest of the narrative in that manner.

Acknowledgments

Many thanks to my wife, Penny R. Peterson, for sharing me with my various computers and giving up chunks of "our time" for me to write. Thanks also to Patricia Wallenburg, who has done an excellent job making this manuscript into an attractive and readable book. Also appreciate the work of Judy Duguid who provided the skill to clean up an often-difficult style of text communication into a string of words that others can appreciate and read without sacrificing my unique voice and style of expression. Immense credit and thanks are also due to my former pastor and friend, the Reverend Dr. Frank G. Ciampa for his review of this text and helpful comments. Thanks to Arianna Montgomery of ADM Custom Art, Prints & Design at admcustomart@gmail.com for her contributions to the book's cover design.

Lucky to Be Lutheran:
101 Reasons

REASON #1. We Lutherans believe the Bible is the inerrant word of God, that is to say, the true and inspired word of God. The church uses a more precise term, saying that the scriptures are the *infallible* word of God. Yet there is no need to believe that every single word in the book is "historically" correct or even meant to be history or as interpreted complete with all its original nuances intact in our current form of modern English or Old King James English with all its distinctions from the original Greek, Aramaic, or Hebrew texts. Language, even the same language, changes over time. Our understanding of a word's meaning can change over time. So, there is no benefit in nitpicking every single word and sentence, because odds are you would be wrong. The most important thing to know about the modern Bible, including the books of the Old and New Testament, is that it is not a book about history, although it contains a lot of history; it is also not a book about the biological beginning of people or dinosaurs, and yet it says that God made man and all other things. Some of the texts in the Bible about worldly things are only the headlines. As a Lutheran, the most important thing to know and understand about the Bible is *that the Bible is most simply a book that is about what God wanted you to know about God and that is authored by God.* What God wants you to know about your relationship with Him is contained in it pages as a road map to salvation. It includes all those things God wanted you to know about Him and the free gift of saving grace achieved by Jesus's sacrifice and His propitiation for all sin and this precious gift given to all sinful people. All the important messages in the Bible combine to inform you about the only known pathway to eternal life with God after death. And just so you know, living your life here on earth as a saved soul in the light of what the Bible teaches is also a good thing.

Said another way, from a worldly perspective there is nothing in the Bible that needs to contradict any scientific discovery and nothing learned in science that needs to contradict the central theme and truths in the Bible. The messages of the Bible need no vindication from the study of science. Said still another way, whatever God did before or after the "Big Bang" or whatever He did to create what we can see, touch, and feel is His business, and it will really never matter to you in this life or the next exactly how that was accomplished. The Belgian priest Georges Lemaître (July 17, 1894–June 20, 1966), who originated the Big Bang theory (expanding universe), felt no conflict between his new theory and his religion or his faith. Where is the value in creating controversy between the Bible and science? Science, though, without God would not exist; science does not and cannot contradict what God's word says about God or the path to salvation revealed to us in the pages of the Bible. There is no difference in the meaning that God created the universe, the world, and man even if you consider that the world was created in six earth days or in six passes of any length of earth time or cosmic time. Believe one or the other or both and move on to the much more important matters of perfecting your personal faith and accepting God's will and grace in your life.

Focus on the core message minus the static we are constantly bombarded with in contemporary society. The actual result of creation itself tells a different story. Are you to deny what is there in evidence set before you? You are here, we are here, the earth is here, and we can see the stars. What we humans think about how it all came to be will change nothing. Simply put, the Bible is a book about salvation; it contains some science, some history, some biology, and even some family trees, but nothing in it contradicts the truths of science, nor can any science text contradict the Bible's defined path to salvation for all mankind.

Separate the event of creation from that thought of creation that took place in an instant. What took place in creation is still taking time for everything to take shape as our universe moves through time. It is hard work for us humans to wrap our minds around all that is happening. The physical laws and objects of creation were necessary. Or what is the point of God doing it? Thinking that all the features of our universe are based on the chance of it all coming together in a way that is just right for us to exist is a mental leap to nowhere.

Why would it even take six earth days? The work of creation is amazing and ongoing. As residents in God's universe, our bodies and minds are nothing more than a necessary vessel to carry our souls and learn more about God as we age and grow in God's grace and ultimately one day reach our soul's home in heaven with God. Hidden in the pages of the Bible are enough headlines and details to help you find your salvation and path to heaven, a oneness with your Creator and Savior.

REASON #2. As Lutherans we accept the carved-in-stone messages that Moses brought down from the mountain, messages that are referred to as the Ten Commandments and that provide instructions on how to behave in this earthly life that came right from God. They are not the ten suggestions, as some would want us to believe. More to the point, we believe that the Old Testament passages referred to as the Ten Commandments serve two timeless purposes: They are very basic rules designed to bring to light what it takes to live a Godly life, a life filled with righteousness, with personal integrity, and with loving purpose toward others. In the corporate world your company might call these basic rules or core values. Furthermore the commandments are basic rules for a life lived that will not hurt your neighbor or yourself. They inform us that God is to be feared, trusted, and worshiped.

The second purpose of the commandments is to remind us daily that we have all sinned (broken these commandments in thought, word, and deed), with not one of us succeeding within a lifetime or even a day of perfect behavior in the sight of God. Regardless of whether you view one sin as more grievous than other, the fact remains that you cannot keep the law. Lutherans call the commandments and other Jewish temple rules derived from them the *law*, God's law. Much of our modern-day and historic civic laws and traditions are derived from these very fundamental commandments.

Perfect adherence to the laws of God is out of reach for us. We can try to obey and attempt to try again, and that is all good, but human behavioral perfection is not possible. We must recognize our sin, ask God for forgiveness, and trust that Jesus's life, death, and resurrection as our stand-in in front of God's sentencing court is where our salivation is derived.

REASON #3. On most Sundays and holy days, the Lutheran service and sermons nearly always follow the same pattern. We call it the liturgy, which is just a fancy word from ancient times that means we follow a formula or a standard order of procedure to conduct the worship service. In the Lutheran Book of Worship, there are five Divine Services that our pastors can choose from for any given Sunday. There are also patterns of service for other events and times. This customary use of these predefined services is a demonstration of a traditional Lutheran belief that every element of the conduct of worship should be done in a decent and orderly manner to honor

God. Following one of these five services helps to assure that "decent" and "orderly" occurs. The practice is to use three scripture readings, with the first usually being from the Old Testament portion of the Bible. The second reading, the Epistle, is from the New Testament (post-Jesus) portion of the Bible citing the words of one of the apostles of Jesus. The third reading, the Gospel (Good News), is always from the New Testament and contains words that Jesus spoke to his followers and contemporaries. These readings are connected in theme or thought, one to the next to the next, thereby keeping the worship service focused on Christ and his work of salvation for all. Other parts of the service include corporate (or public) confession followed by an announcement of absolution; the fundamental creeds of our faith: the Nicene Creed, the Apostles' Creed, and the Lord's Prayer; and a general prayer of the church or collect. The hymns include the opening hymn or hymn of invocation, the hymn of the day or sermon hymn, and a closing hymn of praise and may include other hymns. The end of the service is marked by the words of the Benediction. When Holy Communion is included in the service, there is a standard Service of the Sacrament that follows shortly after the sermon, the prayer of the church, and the offering.

The sermons too almost always follow the same pattern in their message and delivery law followed by the Gospel. The pastor does his best to convict you of your sin, then to not necessarily condemn you for it, but certainly to remind you that the law is still in effect. These are the few—sometimes too few, sometimes too many—moments where you are meant to feel bad about being a sinner. These few moments are moments where some weak in their faith fail to like being a Lutheran or being in the pew when they can see their own sin is at the center of the discourse. All too often what is said by the pastor hits home. The pastor is talking about you (me), and you do feel the emotion of your failure and stubbornness. I know that some have left the Lutheran Church over these events; some have left, going to any other Christian church over the few paragraphs of conviction and condemnation. So, to be a Lutheran you have to accept the doctrinal statement "that all have sinned and fall short of the glory of God." You cannot be a hypocrite and expect to flourish in the Christian faith as a Lutheran. "God, please have mercy on me, a sinner" is your prayer mantra at this point in the sermon. There is nothing uplifting or happy about being a sinner, one who has acknowledged and recognized his or her sinful nature. During the third section of the sermon, now that you're convicted and condemned by the work of the devil, the preacher reminds you that your own merit would never get you to a state of eternal life with God in heaven. But fear not. The pastor then works his words to convince you that Jesus's saving grace and his work of salvation on the cross at Calvary are strong enough to bring you back, because Jesus, the Son of God, paid the price for your sins sufficiently for you to be marked as one of his, a saint. His resurrection on the very first Easter morning is the proof bringing you Christ's forgiveness. As a hearer of the sermon, it is your responsibility to listen fully, to pay attention to both the law and the Gospel in the message.

I am lucky to be a Lutheran because I hear this message nearly every week, accept these tenets to be true, and thank God every day that He provided a way for us to be and remain His, our many sins notwithstanding.

REASON #4. We can respond to the question "Are you saved? . . . Are you born again?" with an unqualified YES. And then recite our baptism date as an infant in most cases. Those that ask are typically from denominations that believe that there is some work of faith, some action, that is necessary on your part for you to be saved. They are also surprised when you can recite the date of your Holy Baptism.

Engaging in some action or work of faith to receive salvation is a far cry from what we believe as Lutherans; we trust that the work of eternal salvation is God's work, Jesus saving us. Salvation is a gift that we simply accept as if it were an inheritance from a rich uncle. We can reject the gift, but there is no merit on our part that brings it to us. Rejecting the gift of salvation is perhaps the worst sin, the unforgivable sin that puts us back under the law and condemns us to a Godless eternity. In Luther's words this is the "grace alone," God's undeserving love expressed for us to mark us as one of His own at our baptism with water and the Word.

REASON #5. We accept that one only needs one baptism for the remission of sins. No need to go into the dunk tank or the river every couple of weeks or every time you change churches or when you commit a grave or mortal sin. Doing so would deny the power of God and obliterate the trust we should place in his Holy Word. Typically, parents bring their newborn babies at six weeks, more or less, to be baptized into the Lutheran faith as newly born Christians. We accept that the combination of water and the Word are both required. It is a washing away of original sin: Man by nature is a sinful being, and in Holy Baptism we are washed free of that sin and made clean, purified, and robed in white in the sight of God. As Lutherans where there are extenuating circumstances, any one of us can perform a baptism using water and these same words from the Lutheran Service Book, pages 268–271.

REASON #6. We believe there is a universal Christian church, the body of true believers that live on the earth as saints and others that are already saints in heaven. The believers who make up this community are in a visible and physical church and at the same time are members in an invisible universal spiritual church composed of all who profess that Christ is their Savior and are baptized. By having this tempered to God's will in our belief, we admit that our own church's doctrine may not be completely perfect in every way, that our own church is perhaps not the only one that can bring a person to salvation, and that others, from other Christian churches can be and are recipients of the gift of grace and salvation by accepting salvation as the gracious gift of God. Only those who totally reject the saving message and work of salvation through Jesus are condemned and have no chance at eternal life with God if their hearts are hardened against the Gospel message of this free-to-all gift.

REASON #7. Lutherans are free and correct to refuse memberships in many social groups on religious grounds. When we are asked to join any organization that has any hint of religion in its ceremony and assembly, we can say "Thank you, but no, it is against my religion" to those invitations should we ever get them. Thankfully any group or organization with a "grand" or "benevolent" anybody in charge is out of bounds for us. We tend to stay clear, and rightly so, of any organization that features rudiments of religion or royalty in its repertoire. Any organization run in the fashion of a lodge, which denies the triune God of Christianity, or one with a man or woman in charge who is referred to as a "grand" anything, or organization that teaches, preaches, or acts in a manner of works righteousness and conducts religious or religious-like ceremony is out of bounds for us. No matter how much good these organizations are reported to accomplish. Any teachings implying that your good works will earn points with God toward your salvation we reject. We believe we are responsible for doing good works only out of thankfulness for Jesus's work of salvation. It is our response to God's love for us, earning us no merit.

On a personal level, if you think about it, any organization where you have to buy your membership, fellowship, and friends is not the kind of organization that will enhance and help build your faith. Think about it for a minute: It is not a good thing to "buy" friends, because they are usually not affordable or friends.

REASON #8. Luther is reputed to have said "Sin boldly," and we do. We sin—not because we are totally evil or are hypocrites at heart; nevertheless we sin because we suffer from the same human frailties as anyone else. It is not that we seek to bring sin into our lives. We just know we won't be condemned to hell if we simply repent, meaning we turn around and face God and seek forgiveness of our sin and renewal in our life. Whenever possible for those deeper sins against others, we should also attempt to make things right. For those sins that mostly affect us, internally drawing us away from God, we should endeavor to do better, to walk closer in the way of righteousness. We are not freed from the worldly consequences of our sin; we are freed from the conviction and sentence to hell because God will forgive our sins, all of our sins, through Jesus's saving work on the cross at Calvary. The most notable words of Luther were in regard to our salvation being gained through "grace alone, faith alone, scripture alone." We trust in that premise and promise.

REASON #9. We love attending our potluck lunches and dinners in the basements and fellowship halls of our churches. These gatherings of fellow believers are one of the ways that we Lutherans spend time getting to know our fellow Christians, just as early Christians have and throughout the ages up to today. We enjoy experiencing fellowship with those who are closest to us in our shared belief system about Christ, God the Father, the Holy Spirit, and the Bible. A shared coffee, a pinwheel sandwich, a slice of vegetable-bacon-egg quiche, and a piece of *apfelkuchen* (German apple cake) and a cup of coffee go a long way to starting a new friendship or ratifying an old one. This gathering around food in some way reflects gathering at the altar for Holy Communion. It is outward confirmation that we are a community of believers in the core Gospel message that Christ died for our redemption from the power of sin that would have dammed us to an eternity without God.

So, each of these gatherings has the potential to become a celebration with fun, food, and fellowship of this gift of God's grace cast onto each of us. These gatherings can set in our minds the sharing of friendship and fellowship that we will experience when we are with God in His heaven. The time spent in the church basement or fellowship halls reminds us that the people we sit shoulder to shoulder with or stand face-to-face with are also God's redeemed children. We are reminded that they make up our "church" family, each one contributing to the other's well-being in some way. This isn't to say that everyone in the hall is going to like, love, or appreciate every other person in the hall at that moment or that week equally. As with any family, perfection in these relationships is not perfect, and when those relationship blips occur, it is a reminder that we are all sinners in need of constant feeding of the Gospel to our hearts and minds in the same way we are in need of physical food and drink to nourish and refresh our bodies. We are in need of Holy Communion to refresh our souls. When there are ripples in a relationship, sitting together over coffee and kuchen at least provides a neutral atmosphere to talk and work past those things that prevent us from fully appreciating each other as a brother or sister in Christ.

REASON #10. **We have the Large and Small Catechism available to read and to enhance our understanding and find a deeper meaning in our relationship to Christ.** These guides contain what Luther thought was fundamental to hearing and learning God's word in the family setting. Essentially learning what is necessary to keep the faith and keep our lives on track. These every day, easy-to-read, and easy-to-understand texts are a part of the larger collection or treatise on Lutheran beliefs called the Book of Concord (Confessions of the Lutheran Church). It contains the three early church creeds (the Apostles' Creed, the Nicene Creed, and the Athanasian Creed) and the documents dated to the Reformation, including the Augsburg Confession, the Apology of the Augsburg Confession, the Treatise on the Power and Primacy of the Pope (all three attributed to Philip Melanchthon), the Smalcald Articles (by Martin Luther), the Small and Large Catechisms (authored by Martin Luther), and the Formula of Concord (attributed to J. Andrease, N. Selnecker, and M. Chemnitz). All these documents are in the public domain and can be found online. They can also be purchased in hardcover book format for under $40 from Concordia Publishing House. You can never know too much about your faith, so these texts will go a long way to help with that lifelong learning for the motivated layperson. Fortunately knowing all this material in not necessary for salvation.

REASON #11. We have a gem in Concordia Publishing House. Concordia Publishing House (CPH.org) is an extension of the Lutheran Church–Missouri Synod and offers everything from commentary books on the books of the Bible, children's books, books on historical theology, and books by Lutheran scholars both sainted and contemporary, to Luther studies and practical theology and much more. Every Lutheran home should have Luther's Large and Small Catechism and the Book of Concord and a Bible, preferably at least one with a modern language interpretation. The King James translation of the Bible reads beautifully, but contemporary English has moved past a lot of the language, and our understanding of the words in King James's time is not what it would be if we lived and conversed in 1611 when it was first published. In other words, obtain something other than the King James Version because we really do not talk that way anymore. A great one to purchase for a serious student of the Bible is called the Lutheran Study Bible, English Standard Version, and is available from CPH.org. The compact paperback edition is under $40 at this writing.

REASON #12. Our salvation is no joking matter, but you will still hear a decent joke from time to time from the pulpit. Lutheran preaching of the Good News (Gospel) is not always fire and brimstone serious, thank God for that. Who could stand leaving church services each week with a heavy heart and the feeling that you have no chance, you will never measure up, and you are doomed to hell when you die and destined to live a hellish life on earth. The "you are saved" message has to transcend both the humor and the brimstone fires, and thankfully most every Sunday in every one of our churches that message is clear: You have the freedom to live your life in a way that only the knowledge of salvation (you are saved) will provide.

There are many things—including traditions, ways of doing things—that are expressed in various religious denominations. Many of these traditional memes, the ones that focus on condemnation, have absolutely nothing to do with whether or not you are going to be saved. You can wrap up all fire-and-brimstone sins in a tidy little bag because in God's eyes sin is all the same. There is no workable grading scale for our sin. We failed to uphold the *law*. A preacher who is being deadpan serious every Sunday and wrapping the churchgoers in the ropes of their sin week after week is not reflecting God's love for us in any way. God seems to me to have a sense of humor because He saved us anyway.

REASON #13. Tithing is an option—sort of. We are instructed that God expects us to share some of the bounty He has shared with us, but not out of duty or cringing fear. We may have worked for all our resources as well we should, however rich or poor we are, but everything we have is a gift from God. And it's not "Let's make a deal" time either when it comes to stewardship. We respond to His generosity and kindness to us with a willing heart and give out of a sense of love and appreciation, compelled to do our bit to support the local church and the greater mission and grow the Kingdom of God because we want to as our response to the gift to us that matters most, our salvation. We give because we want to . . . not because we have to. There is no eleventh commandment that says give 10 percent to the church. Giving whatever percentage or special gift that suits you is fine. Not giving at all, that's not fine.

REASON #14. Our message and church memberships are open to all to hear and for all to participate. Although most Lutheran churches in the United States and Canada are predominantly white and consist of people of German, Finnish, or Scandinavian descent, we are not racists, bigots, or misogynists—or any other negative "ists" for that matter. The door and the Gospel messages are available to all willing participants on a Sunday morning in any of our churches. There is no need to separate those sitting in the pews by categorization other than sinners and those redeemed-by-the-blood-of-Christ sinners. When God looks at any congregation sitting there to worship on Sunday, this is all He sees, and God willing, this is all we see—that is to say, fellow humans, fallen and sinful humans, who are there to receive and to be assured and reassured of the redemption completed for all sinners on the cross of Calvary. Two things happen when you use divisive terms for other people's traits who are not exactly like yourself. First, someone is made lesser and another is viewed as special or privileged. Next, stemming from this line of thinking, this division leads to destroying the concept of fellowship and being in community with one another. When that sense of fellowship and community is diminished by any senseless divisional category that has been applied, all the members of the congregation lose out; they lose out on what is possible when God's love and concern, and the sheer joy and celebration of knowing that you and those next to you are saved, is shared among your church family. There is no feeling equal to what you get from this gift from your Savior of sharing space, time, and a common understanding of this religion with fellow believers of all outwardly descriptions. In a more liturgical sense, this is the communion of saints: the joining of all believers into one tribe dedicated to the furtherance of the Kingdom of God, not dividing or diminishing our human lives or individual characteristics in any way.

REASON #15. We mostly practice close communion, not necessarily closed communion. This is perhaps the second most confusing concept for those not familiar with the practices of Lutheranism in the Missouri Synod to understand. Let me attempt to explain this belief and practice in simplest possible terms. Perhaps using different terms would help. *Open* communion is a practice where anyone in attendance on Sunday can partake of communion, sharing the bread and wine. *Closed* communion would be more accurately described as communion given exclusively to LCMS members and members of those churches in full pulpit fellowship with LCMS. *Close* communion would be communion restricted to only baptized Christians who believe what we believe. This latter kind of communion is fairly difficult to discern on the fly, considering the details.

During the Service of the Sacrament of Communion, we begin with traditional phrases starting with the Preface, next the Proper Preface, the Sanctus, a Prayer of Thanksgiving, and the Lord's Prayer, and then finally the pastor recites the words of Jesus from the very first Christian celebration of communion. When these words are spoken, we believe that in, with, and under the bread and wine that the bread becomes one with the body of Christ and the wine in the same fashion becomes the blood of Christ shed on Calvary for our sins. This is happening in a supernatural way that we don't and really don't need to understand, in much the same way that Jesus incarnate and holy became the God-man Jesus that walked among us in a mystical union. This is different from believing that the bread and wine are completely transformed to be Jesus's body and blood by the words spoken over by the officiant and also is different from believing the bread and wine are not holy in any way and that communion is just a remembrance ceremony of the first-ever Lord's Supper. Lutheran belief is that Jesus is fully present and the bread and wine are fully present.

After the words are spoken come the Pax Domini, then the Agnus Dei, and finally the distribution of the host and wine to the believers. After the distribution we sing the Post-Communion Canticle and hear the Post-Communion Collect, followed by the Benediction. A final hymn is often sung, concluding the service.

So, when we say close, we mean we commune with and invite those who are close to us in our beliefs about Christianity. Close to us in our beliefs about the Sacrament of Holy Communion to commune with us and exclude those who are not; hence the often-misapplied label of "closed" to outsiders. What the message is, what it should be is you as a visitor may be welcome to commune with us but not yet, not without some level of conversation or instruction and acceptance of that closeness of beliefs by meeting briefly with the pastor of that church or the pastor who is the one in charge of exercising pastoral care to congregation members and their families and friends.

Some of our conservative congregations do practice closed communion, exclusive to LCMS and to those churches in fellowship with us. At this writing there are 38 other church bodes in full altar and pulpit fellowship with the LCMS. Three of those are in North America, and the rest are in Latin America, Europe, Asia, and Africa. An LCMS pastor is allowed to question and discuss this belief about communion with people from other Christian denominations wishing to commune at one of our services, and the pastor is allowed to grant pastoral care access to Holy Communion at the church he is called to or in extenuating conditions, such as when serving as a hospital chaplain.

Changing this practice would present a great risk of providing a bad example that could destroy the integrity of the faith over time and diminish communion to just a remembrance ceremony or less.

This management of access to communion is nearly always covered in the service bulletin, a disclaimer if you will. The service bulletin advises visitors to meet with the pastor or an elder of the church prior to the service for those wishing to commune for the first time when visiting. As one who has visited more than my fair share of congregations, the tone of wording of the bulletin notice matters. Some can be projected in a way that is quite offensive, although that is not the intent.

At one church I visited early in my adult life, there was no time to talk to the pastor before the service, and I was quizzed right at the altar during communion about my church affiliation, my confirmation date and place, the name of the church of which I was a member, and the date and place of my baptism. If you had my memory for historical events, particularly dates beyond getting the year right and maybe the month, you would likely appreciate how uncomfortable this might have been for me. Got through the inquisition OK and fully understood why he did this, because I remembered the lines from 1 Corinthians 11:27–29.

This is not necessarily a good thing for some first-time visitors and is possibly a detriment to increasing the membership of LCMS congregations from the visitor pool, at least with people from other denominations that do not take Holy Communion as seriously as we do. Our communion practice is modeled from these Bible passages:

1 Corinthians 11:28 (self-examination)
1 John 1:9 (baptized and sorry for my sin)
Romans 5:9–11 (Jesus paid the penalty for my sin)
Matthew 26:26–28 (I receive fully bread and wine and
    simultaneously fully body and blood of Christ Jesus)
Romans 12:2 (I resolve to accept God's will)
1 Corinthians 11:27–29 (for those who understand its pur-
    pose and meaning)

So, we say those who believe these principles are welcome to commune with us. Therefor the "close" mantra best defines our practice, those who are close or in sync with us in our belief about the Gospel and the Sacrament of Communion.

Some interpret this as closed communion, which in a way it is. By close communion we mean we partake of the Lord's Supper with those who are close to us in our set of beliefs, not only about communion, but about the path to God's salivation (as defined succinctly by Martin Luther's quote "grace alone, faith alone, scripture alone"). The Sunday morning bulletins contain what is essentially a disclaimer stating why an unknown visitor may be denied the bread (wafer) and wine (cup or glass) at the altar. Although the disclaimer wording varies a little from one church to another, the essence of the statement and warning is the same. Visitors are always encouraged to and should consult the pastor or a church elder or deacon before communing for the first time.

REASON #16. It only takes a minute to convert to Christianity as a Lutheran, but it takes weeks to confirm the conversion unless

you are dying. If you die right after your conversion (classic deathbed conversion), then your further lessons come from those most qualified to teach on the other side of the curtain of death. Jesus was able to take the thief on the cross into heaven without giving him a lot of instruction. Not exactly a deathbed situation, but the concept is the same. Here on earth, to convert to being a member of the Lutheran Church, you have to go through youth confirmation (for two years typically), or adult membership classes for six to ten weeks, or many conferences with a Lutheran pastor depending on your past religious beliefs and experiences. The bottom line is that the church does not want you to be ill-informed about what you should believe with certainty and those false teachings you should categorically reject. You must know with confidence those things essential to our faith and what provides your salvation. There is a passage in Acts (2:41) that states that those who heard the apostle Peter accepted his message and were baptized, and about 3,000 were added to their numbers that day. Might have been a wordy sermon and taken some time out of the day, but the point is, it was happening in the course of a single day. In Acts 4:4 the report is that there were 5,000 new believers in spite of Peter and John being detained. Regrettably, conversions to Christianity are not happing at anywhere near that pace today. Not only do nonbelievers need the conversion, but people who lived a whole life in the Christian faith need reassurance of that redemption. I remember holding the hand of a centenarian plus three years as she was preparing to pass on in a nursing home, within the hour as it turned out. She asked, "Dennis, do you really think Jesus will forgive my sins?" I reassured her, "He will," and she smiled for her very last time on this earth.

REASON #17. Women can serve as commissioned deaconesses, as full-time professional church women. In the LCMS, women are not ordained as called ministers or pastors. Some would find this a problem, as there is evidence that a woman named Priscilla played a critical, but not pastoral, role in the first 70 years of the Christian church. Paul spoke of her and her husband as "fellow workers" in Christ. Mary Magdalen was the original messenger of the news that Jesus had risen from the dead, followed by Mary the mother of James, Salome, and Joanna, then the apostle Peter. There are many other roles that women can occupy within LCMS churches; it is just that the fatherly role of pastor is not accepted within our doctrine and practice because of a lack of certain scriptural support for the concept. That does not mean that the roles women do fill are not meaningful and furthering the Kingdom of God by sharing the Gospel message in thought, word, and deed. My own mother was an influential volunteer Sunday school teacher most of her adult life who instilled the word of God in her students by teaching and by her example. Some of her middle school Sunday school students became pastors in the faith. Ordination is not a prerequisite to study more of God's word and to use that knowledge to minister, to preach and teach, to guide or counsel others in learning the Gospel message and receiving it into their hearts. Fortunately, not being able to be an ordained pastor is in no way a showstopper for any woman or man wanting to share the faith, bring someone into the faith, or nurture someone along the path to salvation.

REASON #18. Our pastors are considered to be God's agent on earth for the flock they serve, but they are not God, not divine, and certainly not holy. They are every bit as human as you and I. Said another way, there is no ring kissing or bowing to another man going on in the Lutheran Church, not within the ranks of the ordained or between laypersons and pastors. We hold our ministers in reverence only for the message they bring and out of respect for the called office they hold in our churches, not because of who they are or their extensive education or purported closeness to God. We accept that their position or behavior does not make them holy. They too have sinned and do sin daily and are in need of the forgiveness offered by Christ on Calvary just as much as we are in need. Having said that, we can still take the idea and recognize that our ministers probably work harder at obeying the laws of God, adhering to the commandments more than we laypeople do. They have to carry the added burden in their behavior that their public sin reflects negatively on the universal church, the Gospel message, and the local congregation they serve. That is true of a layperson's non-saintly behavior too, but not necessarily to the same degree.

We Lutheran Christians and our pastors, however, are all saints, even Saints with a capital S. So may you be—that is to say, once you have heard and accepted this Gospel message as true: that God sacrificed his Son that all who believe will be saved out of God's own grace for us, never by our own merit. So as believers, we too are no different from those who have crossed the curtain of death before us; we too are his saints on the earth and joined through that same grace to those who are with God not on this earth yet nonetheless in heaven.

REASON #19. We have the Lutheran Hymnal to enhance our services, actually a few of them. The Lutheran Hymnal has been a staple in church pews in America since 1941, this early one having the famous page 5 and page 15 Divine Services so often used until the Lutheran Book of Worship showed up in 1978. Many congregations had a hard time getting away from the 1941 version with its elegant prose sited between lines of music that will light up a pipe organ. The newer renditions, six of them, of service books and hymnals all attempt to bring a modern note to the worship service, and the verses contain words in some of them that are more in common use today. The common thread through all these hymnals is that the hymns, whether traditional, contemporary, or more modern, are biblically and doctrinally sound for Christian teaching and praise for the most part.

REASON #20. CPH publishes a booklet called the Portals of Prayer for conducting a guided daily prayer life. This little book, written by a combination of pastors and laypersons in and close to the church, is intended to provide a person or a family an easy-to-use focal point to incorporate our faith and learning into our home prayer and worship life every day away from the church building. Published each quarter and available at most all LCMS churches, it offers up daily a short Bible reading, commentary, and prayer line for every day. This daily devotional guide includes an order of family devotion, Martin Luther's daily prayer regimen, mealtime prayer, scripture reading, a discussion, and a prayer for each day of the quarter. Special prayers can be found at the back of the booklet. The only prerequisites for use of the Portals of Prayer are a willingness to use it and the ability to read, or hear. One-year subscriptions are available from Concordia Publishing House priced between $15 and $20 a year. It is also available in Spanish, in braille format, and on cassette tapes. The idea for its use in the family environment is for fathers, mothers, or the head of the household to gather the family together at a regular point in time each day, such as after supper or before bedtime, for sharing and following the devotional material. Besides the benefit of great family togetherness time centered on Christ and the Gospel, those with children can become examples of a life of faith, and parents can also use this time to learn what their children are thinking and dealing with in their lives away from the house. When these devotions are conducted in a loving, caring way, it can keep families close, mend wounds in the family fabric, and bring about Christ-centered lives in adults and children. Along with attending church regularly, reading the Bible at home, and centering your own life as a Christian, there are few better ways to pass this gift of salvation to family members than having a Christ-centered, family-centered daily devotional time in your home. The Portals of Prayer will get you there with ease and can keep you there.

REASON #21. That wonderful highbrow-sounding word "adiaphora"—we mostly understand what it means. If a singular something exists in the practice of religion that is not demanded or forbidden by the Holy Scriptures, it is said to be an "adiaphoron." In other words, doing the practice or not does not impede or improve the path to salvation. There are things that have crept into the practices exercised by our Lutheran congregations that fall into the category of adiaphora. One simple example might be the color of the advent candles; another would be the date for putting up or taking down a church's Christmas tree. There are many others. Also, things from our personal lives might fit the description, such as knowingly speeding down the expressway might be considered adiaphora. However speeding, it might speed your journey to heaven. Many of those overly embraced practices in some congregations are traditions that have come into existence since Luther's time and later. When any church member refers to something as "We have always done it that way," that is a clue you might be dealing with an adiaphoron-related topic. It is really OK to take down the Christmas tree before, on, or after Epiphany, except for the fact somebody in the congregation is going to care and let you know he or she cares.

REASON #22. We are in nearly all circumstances morally opposed to abortion, but not the girl that "got in trouble" or the

mom that had to make a tough decision about her own survival. Forgiveness is available here. Rape happens all too often among the high school–age and college-age population. On top of that, kids and young people do stupid things without enough of a discerning thought, being in charge of their all too emotional brains that lead to taking actions and risks that are not in any way problem-solving behavior. Unwanted pregnancies are a fact of life now as in the past. The big difference now is that many of these instances of unwanted pregnancies become abortions that can be avoided. Another difference in our current world is the universal availability of no-questions-asked abortions and a deterioration of our moral fabric as a nation that thinks killing babies is to be OK.

Lutherans and Lutheran churches and Lutheran Social Services stand ready to help unwed mothers in so many ways. One of my friends and her husband were fortunate enough to be able to adopt two children over the course of three years thanks to the work of Lutheran Social Services and two unwed mothers who were able to choose life over abortion. There are tens of thousands of couples like my friends more than ready and anxious to adopt.

Lutherans for Life is a proactive organization that needs support on a local and global level. This organization focuses on the sanctity of life from conception to natural death. Visit http://www.lutherans forlife.org to learn more about this organization.

We can pitch the moral strength to the young along with advocating abstinence. Yet when that fails, those who stumble need to be embraced as redeemable children of God by each of us.

REASON #23. My mom was a Lutheran first. Families with one parent with his feet in the door of one church and the other parent with her feet in the door of another church can work out. It cannot be optimal though for a child trying to sort out why mommy's faith is different from dad's faith. The point here is that I was fortunate enough to grow up in a loving, nurturing Christian home where the whole family went to a Lutheran church service on Sunday. I was allowed to make mistakes, learn from them . . . build my own character in an environment that was loving and supporting. It was my mother's Christian beliefs in action that made the quality of my early childhood development possible.

The old saying goes that either you are setting the example or you are the example. Meaning that as a parent or guardian, you are living a God-fearing life, and it shows sufficient for your children to pick up on it and make it their own way of dealing with a sinful world; or alternatively you are providing the example of a Godless sinful life, and kids get caught on to that reality right away. I grew up financially poor and fatherless, and I experienced a lot of peer influence going against my "turning out OK." None of that mattered, because in our home the Christian love and acceptance showed through in everything I experienced as a child in my family and as a child of God attending church regularly.

REASON #24. Lutherans accept that God is really the only one who can make true "doctrine." All we do, preach, or regulate in the church has to be subservient to that thought: God's word holds the truth about him and our relationship to him and our place and role in this world. Ordinary men or women cannot create doctrine. They can try to find new ways to explain doctrine; however, this can become a slippery slope to grievous errors. Our scribes, religious scholars, professors, and pastors can dig into the Holy Scriptures to find facts and truths, but they are not allowed to add ideas to it or make up their own humanistic interpretations. Our belief is that when the words of the early scripture were written, the men who wrote them (the prophets of old and the early apostles) were inspired by the Holy

Spirit to create these writings for the edification of the audience they faced in their own time and for the audience throughout time to the present day. The messages will benefit all the future readers of the Holy Scriptures as well. Each successive generation has the opportunity to learn anew the very same message of God's love leading to our redemption that was taught in the church during its first 100 years, and reaffirmed after the Reformation, or revolution if you prefer. The Protestant movement burgeoned in 1517 to send that message all over the known world and into the present time, and our sincere prayer is that tomorrow's believers will hold fast to the same simple truths contained in the Holy Scripture.

The problem with the concept of any new interpretation of the scripture is that we are removed from the original language, removed from the context and culture where the original languages of the scriptures were used both in the everyday speech of the time and in the scholarly writings of the period. The second problem with new interpretations is that the meaning and use of words in any language change over time. These Holy Spirit inspired earthly authors of the Bible texts captured the intent of what they were thinking into writing. What we as Christians need to know is included in that scriptural intent; that intent is what is the accepted shared Christian/Lutheran doctrine. It is what we believe to be true about God, and what is true about our relationship to him. We can be close to that intent in our doctrine, and close is probably good enough, as the core message of how our salvation happens is not that complicated by design.

REASON #25. We actually talked about and learned about the Ten Commandments in seventh and eighth grade confirmation class in a manner that left us without the feeling that we are all doomed to hell. The Gospel message is always the same in the Lutheran Church, fortunately always the same. We were taught all the relevant issues of our sinful nature in a straightforward way. We were also taught that God's plan since Cain killed Abel was that God would send a Savior to redeem all of mankind. The classic second chance for humankind. We learned that we all sin and that we are forgiven when we repent and are sorry for our sins. Perfection in God's eyes is not possible for humans; God does see us covered, redeemed by the sacrifice of his Son, Jesus. Some say spare the rod and spoil the child, and bring up children in the way that they should go, that way being to follow the commandments. There is a difference between bringing up children as God fearing only, as opposed to God fearing *and* God respecting, meaning that God is expecting discipline and restraint from sinning but still has the capacity to love us as sinners. We can be welcomed back into the fold of God's grace when we repent and do our best to amend our life by doing our best to refrain from further sin. The bottom line for us and our children to know is that they sin, we sin, but God's redemptive power through Jesus works for us anyway. The Ten Commandments I learned are not God telling us what to do or not do as a way of controlling our lives; it is God telling us we do sin as we go about living our lives.

REASON #26. **There are conservative (traditional), liberal, and what I call "daring" scholars as pastor-preachers in the Lutheran Church.** The ones I admire most, the brave ones, are those who may not follow every nuance of their seminary training, who realize that they too hold the same educational credentials as many of the professors they had at seminary and can often look at the Biblical, historical, and language evidence and reach an inspired conclusion that is not in 100 percent alignment with the church's peripheral Lutheran doctrine and dogma on a given subject or text. Some things are steeped in tradition and mired in the educational system so deeply that some people tend to take certain things for granted as truth, when maybe, just maybe, there is a misconception going on there. If not, what is the point of any more scholarly Bible research and learning? Everything you need to know about your salvation may fit on the back of a cereal box or in a sewing thimble, but that simple knowledge and message is not always enough for every individual believer. Many Christians are thirsty for learning every aspect and nuance of the faith. Fortunately for them, we have what I call these few "brave" scholars, because they are sort of in the pattern of Martin Luther himself, not really wanting to overthrow the church's doctrine but to fine-tune our understanding of it just a bit. Praise them is all I say, but I fully understand that the greater danger is posed by the liberal ones who move too far with the times (away from the Bible) and deep into our politically correct culture, and move with and agree to our social upheavals without any evidence from the Bible that doing so might be OK. The central message of salvation cannot be diluted and reconstituted to suit every whim and current fancy; still, there is room to improve our understanding and knowledge to benefit those thirsting for it.

REASON #27. It is OK to skip Bible studies from time to time or not go at all. You won't lose your church membership if you miss Bible study or never go at all. No sin involved there, yet going regularly affords the attendees several benefits. The reason it is OK not to go at all is partly because if you go to church on Sunday regularly, depending on the worship schedule used by your pastor, you will hear most of the Bible's important bits in a year or in three years as part of the regular church worship service. You will hear the most important readings from the Old Testament and New Testament in what we refer to as the Old Testament Reading, Epistle, and Gospel. Pastors will frequently also share other bits from the Bible supporting the texts that a particular sermon is generally based on. Every Lutheran home should have a dust-free Bible available for all family members to read. A particularly good choice is available from Concordia, and it is called the Lutheran Study Bible. Going to Bible studies, particularly those led by the pastor, are quite worthwhile to learn more of the domain of Christianity. I was told a secondhand story about a talented natural healing advisor and nonbeliever who was asked by an Amish elder to please read through the Bible and then tell the elder about all the plants with healing properties mentioned in the Bible. So, he did read the Bible from cover to cover and wrote about the plants, and I am told that after he finished the project, he became a Christian. That is what is called the "power of the Word." We are encouraged to read our Bibles at home and learn more; we are just not keeping score on it. God might be though.

REASON #28. The local congregation has the means and power to remove a failing pastor. As a congregation, we can give a bad pastor the boot to the curb, so to speak. Stated another way, we called him, and we can undo a call to him also. Our church is not a hierarchical enterprise; each congregation controls its own destiny in many ways. There is no bishop or district president that can override a vote to send a pastor packing who is no longer serving the spiritual needs of the congregation. Pastors can fail; it happens; they are human too and can err. It takes a vote of the congregation to call a pastor as defined in each congregation's constitution and bylaws. It likewise takes a similar vote of the congregation to remove a pastor for cause. Some reasons for removal include neglecting one's duties, teaching false doctrine, living a scandalous life, and exhibiting no ability or motivation to work. Problems also occur when a pastor becomes "overbearing" to the congregation or some group of its members; this is a point where the district president should apply some counseling. Other reasons for dismissal include a physical or mental problem preventing the pastor from carrying out his responsibilities. For example, the secular monetary affairs of the congregation are the responsibility of the elected officers and voters of the congregation. A pastor could get dictatorial about monetary decisions, and doing so to the point of bankrupting could lead a congregation to remove the pastor. Without going through all the examples, suffice to say that a congregation has the legal, moral, and spiritual responsivity to act in such cases. Checks and balances between the congregation members and clergy exist to ensure that the delivery of the Gospel goes on unimpeded in every Lutheran congregation. This places a huge responsibility on the congregation members that is no easy task to measure up to. Scriptural and doctrinal knowledge about the roles and duties of a pastor and compassion must both exist within the congregation to make the checks and balances work out.

REASON #29. We can drive cars and use electricity in our homes and wear jewelry. Not to say here that doing without something as a part of a religious practice is a bad thing. Showing personal restraint and discipline is an admirable quality, particularly when achieved by God-respecting and God-fearing people. As Lutherans we just simply cannot accept that it brings the person or the community any closer to God than someone who does not have this avoidance practice or tradition. Two reasons for that point of view: The first reason is that it limits the power of God and his message of salvation and grace for all believers through Jesus's crucifixion, death, and resurrection. If you believe doing something or not prevents God from extending his grace to you, you then are stepping into the shoes of God to limit his power, which is purely nonsensical. The second reason is that all the things, technologies, inventions, and science on the earth are a gift from God intended for our use and furthering his Kingdom on the earth. We can also eat pork, sauerkraut, and cabbage and drink wine or beer or a martini or two without fear that what food that goes into our bodies will defile us and prevent our passage to heaven. Avoiding excess and living a life marked by moderation is, however, highly valued in Lutheran circles. This all stems from the concept that there is nothing we can do to work our way into or deny our way into heaven, except for denying or rejecting the message of Jesus's sacrifice in our place, for our salvation. Rejecting the message of salvation for all believers will cancel your ticket to heaven. We have Christian freedom, are free to live our lives, make choices . . . make mistakes and sin and be forgiven from that sin. I personally oppose any tradition or line of thought or argument that removes or limits the power of God in any one of his personages.

REASON #30. Communion for Lutheran's does not have to be the "common" (shared) cup. Within Jewish tradition and even in the Bible, there are countless rules about cleanliness. I think it is unlikely that what we call the "Last Supper," regardless of exactly what day it took place, was celebrated with only one cup; more likely, one vessel or one pitcher was probably used to pour the wine into individual cups or chalices, but just one drinking cup shared across all in atten-dance was highly unlikely in my mind. Second thought is, volume in one cup—who would have just sipped only a little wine after the Words of Institution spoken by Jesus as we do today? In my mind it is the words and the bread and wine, just like in baptism it is the words and water, that combine to make the gift holy. The delivery system: chalice or individual cup for the wine and bread/body and blood of Christ, is far less relevant than the communicant receiving the gift itself.

REASON #31. We believe that all Jews, Jewish in both an ethnic and religious context, are not necessarily excluded from heaven.

The Bible tells us that the people of the Jewish race (ethnic) are God's chosen people. That, one would think, has to count for something. It would be hard to accept that the people of Abraham, Moses, David, and Solomon—and Jesus—the ones that held onto and passed God's message to us and carried it across the world and the millennia, would all be categorically excluded from God's plan of gathering his flock back to himself. Yes, chosen has to count for something. Of course, some Jews will say sarcastically, "Chosen for what? Oppression, slavery, to die in the holocaust?" Some of my more liberal Jewish acquaintances have suggested to me that the United States of America, not the state of Israel, is the true "Promised Land" for those of the Jewish faith. Mostly because they can practice their religion here in the USA freely in most cities and towns across this country safely, as well they should. The American-based movement Jews for Jesus is an active organization that works to bring the Gospel message to God's chosen people again both here and in Israel.

REASON #32. There is no pope in our church hierarchy. Our individual churches are a self-governing body of members walking in unison together in our assemblies within congregations and the joining of our respective churches in synod to worship and share the Gospel of Jesus Christ. Our start as Lutherans began partly as the then pope, Pope Leo X, overstepped and miss stepped with his highly visible issue of selling indulgences in Germany, giving rise and focus to other complaints about the church being run like a temporal fiefdom. So as Lutherans, most of us lay members abhor the idea of a centrally run church, district, or synod even if Christ were to set it up that way. The elected district presidents and even synodical presidents may have a tendency to be "bishop-like" in their administration after their election; yet strong leadership based on Lutheran beliefs at the parish level can hold those tendencies in check. In

Lutheran churches, the management is elected; at the regional and English District level, we elect a delegate (a pastor and lay member from each congregation) to meet in district convention to elect district leadership and to study, deny, or pass proposals for change onto the convention of the full synod. Regrettably, some of the current thought is that pastors should act like CEOs of companies at the church level, when the reverse is true; they are called to be spiritual leaders, not business managers. Like all bad and some good ideas in Lutheran practice, this thinking will fade into history, as it lacks biblical support and practicality and acceptance by local parishioners that really do know better. Jesus's disciples started churches all over the regions they could reach, visited them often, and managed the day-to-day affairs of exactly none of them. They also wrote "letters" to the early churches to keep them advised on spiritual matters. Now that spiritual guidance role, that sole role, is the real purview of our modern-day Lutheran pastors.

REASON #33. The good seats close to the front by the pulpit and altar are almost always available when you come in late. As a member or visitor, you can march right up to the front pew to find a seat. Unfortunately, the last time I saw a visitor actually do that, he was totally hammered drunk. This always-available seating does not apply on Easter or for Christmas season services when the poinsettia and lily people show up for service; you know, the ones who come only two or three times a year just to see the flowers. One of the worst thoughts in common culture is that you can worship God anywhere and "commune" with God in nature. Sorry, folks. That is really worshiping nature, not God. There is no other way to worship than to show up at a Christian church service somewhere. One has to realize that corporate church services benefit you, not God. He's going to be just fine if you never walk into a church, but you probably won't be.

Never use being late as an excuse not to show on Sunday; odds are there will be a place for you.

REASON #34. There is no need for us to memorize all the names of the saints of old. We, as believers, are all saints anyway, just residing on one side or the other of the curtain of death, making the task to name them all impossible anyway. Commonly in Lutheran circles the saints of old times are recognized if sainted by the church prior to the Reformation; we even name churches after them with some regularity. My home church was St. Paul's. However sincere our reverence for the well-known saints of the Bible, the New Testament, and early years of the church, we do not endow the apostles and church leaders with any special powers or pray to them, as Jesus is our only intercessor and the only one we need. We also believe that anyone's great Aunt Nellie who died in the faith is a saint in heaven, and we don't pray to her either. We are to revere them and be thankful for the role that all the saints before us played in preserving and advancing the faith over time.

REASON #35. As a tourist or traveler, I can attend any church in the Lutheran Church–Missouri Synod anywhere in the country or other countries and for the most part hear a similar and familiar message on Sunday. Travel to other church congregations yields the same message mostly. We believe that every Sunday someone in the congregation really needed to hear that particular message being preached. We believe that God works in a mysterious way to guide the preacher's words and opens the ears of parishioners, so that those in need of inspiration, solace, or confirmation of faith get exactly what message they really needed to hear, whatever it might be. When traveling or in a new area, many Missouri Synod Lutherans go through a serious process to choose a church in a strange place for

Sunday worship. We do things like use the church directory, check the Yellow Pages phone book, go to the synod website http://locator .lcms.org/nchurches_frm/church.asp, or visit the websites of prospective churches to find a church at which to worship for the Sunday or two we are away from home. We look to see if the church advertises a traditional or contemporary service style, what, if anything, is said about Holy Communion practices, and other details down to which of our seminaries the pastor(s) graduated from. Yes, we are seeking a sameness—a comfort zone—but most of all we wish to hear the Gospel preached and celebrated in its purity as we have come to know it.

REASON #36. Twenty-two minutes is considered a long sermon. I told one of my current coworkers that when I first retired from full-time work, nearly any work at all, I became so busy with life stuff that the only time I had for any rest was in church during the 20 minutes of the sermon. Seriously though, these 20 minutes are not always enough, so it is better to be well rested and to pay attention while you are there. God either will forgive me all the times I did snooze off for not keeping the watch (hearing the word of God) or will consider that the sermon was a message I already had down pat. If not, I am in deeper trouble than I thought and maybe missed out on something important.

Our feeble attention spans are voting on the side of shorter sermons, the 20-minute ones. The 20 minutes a Sunday only add up to 17 hours over the course of the year, a mere 2 workdays of time listening to God's messages to us. Pastors, at least in theory, work all week to bring us that 20-minute message, so any less than 12 minutes can become a disappointment.

Perhaps we would be better off with longer sermons, but it certainly is not our tradition, and so our pastors are constantly challenged to pack as much punch into the short sermon time as they can. Our life outside the church building provides the quiz for us from all the previous sermons. Paying attention for as long as is takes is worthwhile because of the forever constantly coming-at-you quizzes of real life.

REASON #37: We don't really have to give anything up for Lent, but it is OK if we do. The season of Lent is a time where many Christians deny themselves something meaningful or something they enjoy in order to remember and make real Christ's own suffering and denial of self, right up to his saving act on the cross. There is nothing we can do to equal what he went through to bear mankind's sins of the entire world, past, present, and future, in his suffering and death. By volunteering to give up something for Lent, it merely makes us mindful of Christ's own suffering for our sake. The sentence of death for our sin was ours, but he took it on himself to free us from the eternal punishment of our immoralities and sinful behavior. He served our sentence. Symbolism aside, we can certainly be mindful of that all year long without ever giving anything up for a mere 40-plus days out of the year.

REASON #38. Lutherans know peace. We know peace and at times can even feel that peace in our lives wherever and whenever in our physical bodies and conscious and subconscious mind lets us go there. To Christians there are many flavors of peace. Peace of (in) the world, the peace of God; we are at peace with God, peace internal to the fellowship we are in, peace within ourselves brought about *by knowing that our souls are saved.* As a practicing Lutheran you can claim all versions of this peace of God brought about by his saving grace. *The peace from knowing your sins are forgiven* and you are a child of God is unequaled.

One "peace" practice that you will find in some congregations during the Sunday service is "sharing the peace" by saying "God's peace" and shaking hands with those who are seated by us. Often, depending on where this practice is placed during the course of the service, it can seem out of place and disruptive. Some pastors argue that if this practice is going to be used at all, it should follow the pronouncement of absolution, as to be less disruptive to the rest of the service. The practice is supposed to amplify the idea that we are all connected to each other through our kinship with Christ our Savior. I personally don't know if this moment in the service is necessary for us to know that. I'm quite happy to reserve the fellowship with my fellow believers over coffee and doughnuts after the service. Peace, after all, does not come from our neighbors; it comes from God. I discovered one practice I found interesting if not useful when I was helping out on a political campaign and was visiting inner-city churches in Detroit. After the service in one of those churches and the congregation heard the political pitch by my candidate, the entire congregation stood up, exited to both sides of the church, not using the center aisle, and started a "people train" to meet in the center of the altar area and shook hands to share the peace with each other, and then exited down the alternate side aisle. This method connected everyone to everyone else over time; some would go back to share with the people in their own line; others would exit. I remember thinking at the time, "I am not sure we Lutherans like every other Lutheran in the congregation well enough to do that." Still not sure; need a little more of that peace, so we keep going back every Sunday.

REASON #39. Lutherans are thankful for the gift and comfort of using a standard liturgy nearly every Sunday. We generally do not appreciate surprises on a Sunday morning. The familiar pattern of the various services conducted on Sunday morning brings a sense of comfort, continuity, and assurance that the worship service will be conducted in a decent, familiar, and orderly fashion. The roots of this familiar pattern of service can be traced back to the earliest of the Christian church services. The service is scriptural; that is, there are biblical references for every segment of it. Some of the elements of the Lutheran liturgy can be found in the Old Testament. There is a certain comfort and connection in knowing that these service practices reach back to the Jewish religion as expounded on in the Bible and others that date back to the very beginnings of Christianity. One could almost expect that a Christian worshiper from the first century would not be uncomfortable or surprised by the service program in a modern-day LCMS church.

REASON #40. There are many ways we can learn more about being a better Lutheran. The average Lutheran may not be your best source of information about being Lutheran and explaining Lutheran doctrine. I would include myself in that; just a lay guy who knows enough to get by, and knows he can get to spend eternity with God through God's grace for all. Lutherans you meet may be scholarly or can be of the mindset to simply embrace fully and count on what things they already know about their faith. Fortunately for us the core message is not that complicated: God sent Jesus to save us from the eternal consequences of our sin. We, like nonbelievers, cannot escape the earthly consequences of our mistakes and misdeeds.

When you think that people can get PhDs in Lutheran doctrine, there must be a lot more to learn, and there is so very much more. One easy way is to just keep on going to worship services on Sunday or whenever offered. Beyond that there are adult confirmation classes, Sunday school classes, and Bible studies held on Sunday and often during the week on or a weeknight. For self-study there is the compilation in the Book of Concord mentioned elsewhere in this book, the Lutheran Study Bible, any version/translation of the Bible itself, online video sermons from some LCMS congregations, online resources at https://lcms.org, and a myriad of publications available from Concordia Publishing House. LCMS-affiliated colleges and universities are also available for resident coursework. Your Lutheran education journey can take you from just knowing a little more about a particular Lutheran/Christian topic all the way to achieving a doctorate degree.

REASON #41. We strongly embrace the set of principles we try to follow. Our collective success varies on this one and from person to person and as changes in our ability to respond ensue as when helping events and opportunities occur over time. We embrace the idea that we are called to be little lights in the world, to set a positive example for what it means to be a follower of Christ; however, we don't always get it right when it comes to acting out on that principle of "loving our neighbor as ourselves." Sometimes the call to help is answered by the reply, "Why don't they get jobs?" or "Why should I help them? They can work." We embrace the principle with our prayers, teachings, and rhetoric, and yet we are not always on point when opportunities to show that love of God to someone else are right before us. This is one way we know we too are sinners (sins of omission) and in need of God's saving grace in Jesus's gift; thankfully Jesus saved us from our deeply embedded selfishness too. The operative response here to apply to our lives as Lutherans is, I can do that (one thing) even if I can't do everything for those in my family, those in my neighborhood, and those whom I never met who are in need of help. In spite of a reluctant spirit on our part, opportunities to serve God and others are presented to us nearly every day, and just because we failed yesterday does not mean we are doomed to failure today. Sometimes we get to be the hand of God helping someone up, sometimes we get to "teach someone to fish" for their sustenance, and other times we get to give tens, hundreds, or thousands of dollars to someone in need without showing off or expecting a return or even a thank you. A gift is a gift, and strings should never apply to a gift from a Christian. We also can never be satisfied that a monthly donation of $19.95 to some charity, church charity or other, is enough to absolve us from our responsibility to "love our neighbors as ourselves" when that need to help someone slams us in the face in an attempt to destroy our selfishness. We should pray daily to do a better job.

REASON #42. When practiced, the ordination (laying of hands) of our pastors is accepted as tracing back to St. Peter and Jesus in an unbroken line. This is an added point of interest and connection to the past when we are baptized by a Lutheran pastor or confirmed in the Lutheran Church by a pastor that was ordained in this line of succession. We too have been blessed by this gift through many generations who have dedicated their life to the furtherance and continuity of the Kingdom of God on earth. I joke, actually brag about to be honest, that if you shake hands with me, you shake the hand that shook the hand of the Duke (John Wayne). That's because I had the pleasure of meeting him and his daughter when we were taking a private tour of the Country Music Hall of Fame in Nashville. When we are baptized by a called and ordained Lutheran pastor, the line goes back to Martin Luther, through all the previous popes to St. Peter, to Christ himself, and even to John the Baptist. This too is something to boast about, in that through this succession God's grace has been passed to us through his plan and love for us over the generations. It is equally important, no actually more important, to be keeping the doctrine and passing that on from one generation to the next.

REASON #43. It's not about the number of people in the pew.
It is regrettable that our church congregations are thinning out. In most regions of the country, the pews are no longer filled with young and old, with grandparents, parents, and children. The grandparent-aged people seem to be winning the attendance contest, and it is not because they feel their journey to see Jesus on his judgment seat is remarkably close. My opinion is that the influences of the world—particularly the public education system, the "fake" news media, Hollywood and the film and TV industry—have done a great job in their concerted effort, by folly or by choice, to make any and all forms of religion valueless to a younger generation. It is sad, because not everyone is going to be saved. There is a hell, and there is a curse from Jesus in the Bible that says for those who cause unbelief (I am paraphrasing Matthew 19:6): "Better for a millstone to be tied to his neck and he (she) be thrown into the sea." There is hope for the lost, all of the lost; God's book says so. But there is not much left over for people who deny God, deny the saving message of salvation through Jesus, and worse yet cause others to repudiate that message. The millstone the Bible speaks of will not take a naysayer to Atlantis at the bottom of the sea, but it will sink those who deny Christ to hell, to an absence of God in this life and for eternity when their humanistic views cause people to fall away from God.

The better news is that whatever LCMS church that one picks to attend on Sunday morning, odds are there is probably going to be space in a pew for you and your family. We have room and seats for you all!

REASON #44. Private confession is available but rarely required.
Historically—I can say that because I am old enough—historically (still in my lifetime) the Lutheran parsonage was often the place where on Saturday parishioners who felt the need to confess their

sins to the pastor would come and do so before the Sunday Holy Communion service. Corporate confession and absolution have traditionally been a part of the Sunday Lutheran worship service. Luther and Melanchthon both weighed in on the topic in favor of having the options for private confession while always maintaining corporate confession within the Sunday service. It really comes down to the individual believer or communicant; if the person feels the compelling need to confess confidentially to the pastor and receive the words of absolution, he or she can do so by appointment with the pastor. Some churches advertise and offer a schedule for doing so. Fortunately, we believe a contrite heart is all that is required in confession and in receiving absolution regardless of how public or private that sin is. Inserting a pastor between you and God in repenting of your sin does not enhance or limit the power of God to forgive your sins under the light of Christ's work to make you blameless before God. That private confession can lead to help, counseling, or simply affirmation that you are worthwhile regardless of the gravity of your sin and indeed are included in Jesus's redemptive work in spite of your grave sin.

REASON #45. As individuals in the church, we are as responsible for church growth as the pastor is. We are just admittedly not very good at carrying out the focal mission of the whole Christian church on earth. That mission is to make Christian believers out of everyone on this earth by boldly confessing our faith in Christ. Even the simplest of related tasks escapes many us: for example, meeting and making a new friend of the first-time visitor in the parking lot of the church. Carrying out the mission of the church escapes most of us by our not even being willing to identify ourselves as Lutheran Christians at work or in social settings. In the Bible, the Book of Acts to be exact, there are many passages that report on the phenomenal growth rate of Christian believers during the lifetimes and work of Jesus's apostles. All that spreading of the Kingdom of God got done without the aid of e-mail, messenger, social networks, the printing press, the internet, and radio and TV. My thought is, this is why God chose for Jesus, the God-man, to be sent to earth with his message and measure of salvation in those times. At the time of the disciples, it was an enthusiastic person-to-person, or person–to–many listeners, message delivery system. It should be no different today; if you intend to bring someone to the Christian faith, your witness needs to be personal, honest, and enthusiastic.

REASON #46. We are given opportunities to serve in the church, not demands to serve. Within the congregation, in the community, in the nation, and on an international basis, there are countless opportunities to serve the church by ourselves or in concert with others. Beginning with running for an elected church office, being an usher or deacon, or being a volunteer officer.

Many offices in the congregations are elected positions. Regardless of our age, no one is assigning tasks or two-year missions for us. We can participate by giving a few hours or years of our time to a project or tasks that need to be done. The desire to do work to further the Kingdom falls on every heart, but how one carries that out is mostly a personal choice to do or not do. No one will demand we participate in any action or project. A willing, helping hand and heart is the goal. We can volunteer to participate in a number of Recognized Service Organizations (RSOs), LCMS servant events, health ministry, worldwide volunteer opportunities, disaster response teams called Lutheran Early Response Teams (LERTs), and church planting, just to name a few of the many ways we can serve. One only needs to pick one and fully participate in some meaningful way.

REASON #47. The organ music is often something to love. There is hardly anything more inspiring than the sound an old pipe organ with full instrumentation and a stack of keyboards coupled with foot pedals joined with an organist on the bench with a PhD in music playing hymns that have been sung and used in church services for a few centuries. There is one thing better, and that is the one church I attended that has two pipe organs, one in the choir loft and one behind the altar, with two keyboard locations and two accomplished organists on high-church Sundays to play them in tandem—now that is something to behold and appreciate. The liturgy (order of service) and the chosen hymns and music in general are taken seriously in the Lutheran church services. Some of them not always easy to sing, but the organ helps us make those joyful noises to the Lord even with the more difficult and less familiar tunes. A few of my favorites are "Ein feste Burg ist unser Gott," aka "A Mighty Fortress Is Our God" by Martin Luther; "How Great Thou Art"; "Lift High the Cross"; and "I'm But a Stranger Here (Heaven Is My Home)." Contemporary music and bands of all sorts are OK. However, to fully appreciate Sunday worship, a pipe organ, played by a master organist's hands dancing about the keys and feet striking the pedals, rocks the walls with tone and vibration and gives you just a little taste of the sounds of heaven here on earth. I consider myself truly blessed to have grown up in a church with a pipe organ and people who could make its musical offering and praise speak to me in ways that words alone cannot. I also worshiped at another church where the only accompaniment to the hymns was a violinist, also beautiful to behold, and many other churches with a humble piano yet also edifying and moving. All musical instrumentation can bring glory to God and help us feel a little closer to him.

REASON #48. It's OK to have fun at bake sales, church rummage or garage sales, potluck dinners, and other fellowship times. Jesus threw the money changers out of the temple, and so a fine line is drawn about anything involving the management of and reasons for any events in the church where money is exchanged for something in return. Add to that the historical bit about a pope selling indulgences prior to the Reformation; caution always precedes any event involving money being raised in the context of the church through the sale of anything. Certainly, anything resembling gambling is out of the question, with the possible exception of a donation leading to the drawing of a prize for some lucky person. Notwithstanding the prohibition of being viewed as "money changers" or selling the free Gospel in some way, our congregations still manage to have some fund-raising activities that are actually fun to put on and participate in. In the church I was raised in, the Ladies Aid Society put on Sauerkraut Supper (pork, gravy, mashed potatoes, sauerkraut, and apple kuchen and many other sweets) in the fall that was always very well intended and a highlight of the year for many in the local community. This one event funded many of the little mission projects and provided funding to help the church every year with some modest purchases. And the church got a little bit of PR out of the event; at least people knew we existed and where we were located. Some congregations hold the events off-site, but as long as the purpose is made clear and not in violation of our core beliefs, we are allowed to put these events on and participate in them.

REASON #49. In some churches the regulars have assigned seats, sort of. No joke, well yes; but at the very least it is funny. In many congregations there may as well be assigned seats for the longtime members who habitually sit in the same place in the same pews or seats. Not necessarily good or bad in and of itself. You won't find name tags or seating charts, but you will get the occasional stare if you are a visitor and fill someone's space. The displaced "regulars" do get over it, but it takes a minute or two. It's a funny thing about Lutherans, I think, brought possibly about by a biblical verse that says "The first will be last and the last will be first" coupled with the verse that says, and I paraphrase greatly here, "Take the back seat so you can be invited by the host to sit at the head table." Resultingly, the one thing you can count on, barring a wedding or confirmation or some other special Sunday event, is that the front pews or seats will be available for you if you are visiting or arriving late. Maybe this now has become a Lutheran tradition, of sitting in the back of the church first, something that is also possibly brought about by not wanting the pastor to see one sleeping during the sermon. Not really sure how this came to be, not old enough myself to know, but know it has been that way since I was old enough to notice. In any other venue you pay extra for the best seats in the house. We want to be able to be close enough to see the facial wrinkles on the women performers and to count the facial hairs making up a man's mustache or beard during a play performance, "but, oh no, please don't make me get close to the altar or pastor during the service." Filling up the back of the church first is an odd Lutheran quirk, but on the upside, there are a few Bible verses one could argue that support the practice. The upside for anyone running late or being a visitor is that the very best seats are usually available, even one minute before go-time; in the front of the church. Consider yourself invited to the front.

REASON #50. The Lutheran pastors as a rule only try to make you feel really bad about yourself and your sins on one or two service days per year. That would be Ash Wednesday and Good Friday. On Ash Wednesday, some do the imposition of ashes on the forehead, keep the lights down low during the service, and encourage you to leave the service in silence without talking to anyone. Good Friday comes close to that model too, and so worst case as a Lutheran is that you expect to leave church feeling down on yourself only twice a year. Two times are not bad in my reckoning. I have been to services at other denominations that try their best to make you feel bad about being a sinful Christian every Sunday. For me that would be 50 times too many.

REASON #51. You can learn a lot about a church you are visiting for the first time by reading the extra page in the church bulletin. Churches will often have a printed bulletin of the order of service, a newsletter, or just an extra page in the bulletin that has some local congregational information, announcements, or statistics printed in it. As a new visitor, prospective member, or guest of a member, you can pick up a little insight about what this congregation and its leadership consider important. That information might include the weekly-giving financial report, clubs, special events, days and times of Bible studies, services dates and times listings, or youth activities. Whatever might be included provides a snapshot or a glimpse of the character of the congregation. That insight might indicate how active the "church and members" are internal to the church, the community outreach actions it may be engaged in, and perhaps its financial condition. The focus of the work being done inside and outside the church may be well exposed in that "extra" page. Passive "do nothing much" or "maintenance ministry" congregations are likely not using much ink on that page, and churches with a "very active and vibrant activity list" will need a few extra pages to inform members and visitors of all that's happening there. Granted it's not the whole story of the mission, vision, and values of that particular congregation, but it does provide some valuable clues. Your personal comfort within any given congregation is more an indication of your own desired level of engagement than what a church offers to you beyond the reassurance of the Gospel message. Sometimes a quiet congregation is the right place for the highest level of personal growth and learning; and for a fired-up, shiny new Christian, no congregation is going to be too busy for one to feel connected and fulfilled as a worker for the Kingdom.

REASON #52. One of two things, maybe three, is likely to happen to you when you visit a Lutheran church for the first time. Also, and perhaps more importantly, some things will not likely happen at all to a first-time visitor in our midst. Some of those events that are not likely going to happen include the preacher inviting you down for an altar call, or inviting you to come take a bath with us, or asking you to get in the river or tank, or suggesting you see a spiritual or prayer counselor at the back or front of the church. Not knocking these practices; just saying "not for me," To Lutherans, casting discomfort is not in keeping with worship being conducted in a decent and orderly fashion. Our innate fear is making someone else feel uncomfortable during any part of the worship service.

REASON #53. Our pastors can serve as chaplains in the U.S. military branches. There is no prohibition for our members or pastors to serve in the U.S. military. Some of the best parish pastors have been in the military as chaplains or have served in other military officer or enlisted roles. The more a man knows about real life, the more life experiences he has, the better church pastor he can become when doing a second "career" in a parish. One of the most outstanding pastors and theologians I have ever met was an infantry officer in Vietnam and later served as an LCMS chaplain in every armed conflict this nation entered into after Vietnam and prior to 2012, often parachuting into battle zones to serve the troops. Puts a whole new meaning into the Bible phrase "Fear not , , ,"

REASON #54. Our churches have a process for disciplining an errant member to the point of expulsion of a member. This process can culminate in excommunication of a church member. The word "excommunication" itself is descriptive, meaning exclusion from the right to commune with the other members. In order to reach the level of excommunication, the offense, the sin, must be egregious and maintained, or repeated. There are many other references about church discipline other than the process explained in the New Testament Book of Matthew, Chapter 18. When wronged by another member, we are supposed to meet personally with him or her to find agreement. If that does not happen, then bring in another member or church elder to seek resolution. If that step fails, then the pastor and the congregation are joined in the process. The whole idea is to stop the sin and bring the brother or sister, as a repentant soul, back into the fold. This process happens rarely enough in our congregations, that many members do not understand the process. Even after excommunication there is a path back into the fold.

REASON #55. We are thankful for the people we can become friends with within the church. It's nice to know that most all families, couples, and individuals in the church on Sunday morning are God-fearing, family-oriented people and are usually loving and kind people. Friendships at work or at a social club are not quite the same as what is possible with your church friends. We as Lutherans have much different expectations of the behaviors expressed within those friendships held outside the church. If you think about it, with your church family you share the mission of the church, share communion on Sunday, and profess nearly exactly the same set of beliefs about your religion. Fellowship with your fellow church members should be easy and pleasant both inside the context of church functions and outside the church out in the community. To think about these relationships further, these are the folks you will most likely be sharing eternity in heaven with. There is no reason not to enjoy their company now.

REASON #56. Lutheran husbands and wives become one in flesh and one in spirit. Lutheran (or Christian) family relationships are not perfect or far better than those of members of any other religion. However, the model for how marriage is supposed to work in Lutheran households just might be the best model for long-term success in the marriage relationship. Chaos and independence along with selfishness and control-freak manipulation are not representations or descriptions of how marriage should or will work over time. There will always be some disagreement in a marriage, and how those disagreements should be and are actually worked out is what will define a successful marriage and parenting success if children are in the picture. Ephesians 5 offers some insights in verses 22–23. The word in those verses that women object to is "submit" to their husbands as to the Lord. "Submit" is a strong word in our language today; the softer thought conveyed is more of a "give yourself to" or agree. When disagreements occur sometimes, maybe often, the husband will be wrong in a household decision and the wife will have to let him be wrong and maintain peace with that. The hope is that learning will take place. Those same verses direct husbands to "love" their wives in the purest sense of the word. The same advice goes to husbands in a disagreement; the husband also has to show that love and a penchant for peace by letting the wife be wrong from time to time. Wisdom is highly sought after but costly gained. Those married in a church ceremony often raise the act of marriage in their minds to be equal to a sacrament; in any case it is a promise made before God and man to love and care for each other. Even those bound together in a civil ceremony make that same promise directly or implied. Accept in marriage if nowhere else in your life that we are all a work in progress in God's eyes. Husbands and wives, the whole family really, must be strong in presenting to the rest of the world a unified strength derived from the blessings found in harmony at home with the grace of God as its centerpiece.

REASON #57. Because there are about 80 million Lutherans worldwide, we wield some influence in society, governments, and the world, yet do not desire to control governments. This is my way of saying that, other than the right-to-life, antiabortion and anti-mercy killing stands taken by the church and most of its members, we are typically not political or civic cause-of-the-day activists. Not to say there are no strong feelings about the trajectory of government on many current civic issues, because we individually and collectively have feelings about wanting law and order that promotes peace and tranquility in the world we live in. But we are not for taking tranquility at any cost over our principles or morality. It is just not very likely that we are going to assemble in the streets to protest or lobby for making political changes. Our faith for how change should happen rests with the elected leaders and the voters at the ballot box. We exercise our free speech rights in letters or calls to our elected representatives. Our highest civic responsibility as Lutherans is to be responsible stewards of the unadulterated message of the Gospel, to ensure that this message is properly taught and preached in our churches. Furthermore we are responsible for ensuring that the Gospel message is available to anyone who enters through our churches' doors. Our pews are open to Republicans, Democrats, and minority parties equally; we are not of one mind on many civic issues and vote accordingly as individuals. Even on the hot-button issue of the availability of abortion, not everyone agrees. Regrettably, our U.S. legal system failed in *Rowe v. Wade* to differentiate between an abortion that is a medically necessary procedure (to save a mother's life or as a response to rape or incest) and an abortion that is a convenient method of birth control. If the legal system could find laws and rulings to make distinctions between the two, the civic discussions on the topic could be much more informative.

Realistically, we hope and pray that individual Christians make responsible choices in their own lives. I can't help but remember one of the paintings to the right of the pulpit of the church I grew up in. It depicts Jesus the Good Shepherd knocking on the closed wooden door of a building made of stone. Even as a young child, I picked up on the symbolism of this portrait of Jesus to be knocking at the door of your heart and soul (my heart and soul), as if Jesus were to be saying, "Let me in now, so we can rule your heart together." Admittedly for me, perhaps for others, on some Sundays the message of the painting was stronger than the sermon message. So, rather than become activists, we pray that all people in the world would allow Jesus the Good Shepherd to "rule their hearts and minds." When that prayer is answered, civic strife and discord will no longer exist; that would truly be heaven on earth. It is what heaven will be like. Our fundamental belief is that government is the left hand of God, and we pray for laws and policies that are not in conflict with our beliefs.

REASON #58. We collectively pray nearly every week for our elected leaders, the government, first responders, the military, those who are sick, and the continuity of the church. Find the reference for this practice in 1 Timothy 2 and the first seven verses of Romans 13. There are a lot of problems in the world. Problems in families; in communities; in the cities, counties, and states; and in our own country and every country in the world. Not everyone is well; sickness and disease haunt what we call the human condition. We play a role and have a responsibility to do our bit to make the world a little better for others. However, we are not all brain or heart surgeons or world peacemakers. We do what we can, and one of those things all of us can do is pray for the continued success of those who need it and pray for healing also for those who need it. Under the guidance of our pastor or service leader, we pray that God's work will be done on this earth. We pray because God tells us to; we pray because Jesus tells us to; we pray because we have a universal human need to connect with God. Even though God knows our every need and acts to our benefit without our prayer; our prayers of praise, thanksgiving, and petitions for good please him. Our prayers acknowledge his position as Father and Creator. Our prayers express our understanding that ultimately he is in charge of his universe that we are a part of. We pray for the government because we believe that government is figuratively and actually God's left hand at work in the world. The church is his right hand. So as Lutherans we are extremely unlike any religion that presupposes that the government and religion should be one—and do not pray for that; we do, however, pray that leaders, elected leaders, that will govern in a way that pleases God.

REASON #59. Our pastors are quality controlled. Anyone who wants to become a pastor in the Missouri Synod has a pretty high hurdle to jump over and a high hill to climb! First of all, candidates must feel the call to serve God in this way and must really want to be a pastor. They must be communicant members in good standing of an LCMS congregation or one in fellowship with LCMS for at least five years. Second of all, they must be men, men of good character and reputation. There are two paths to ordination; the first step is to obtain a bachelor's degree from any accredited college, for example an engineering degree from Michigan Technological University or a teaching degree from one of the synod's own colleges or universities. With that bachelor's degree in hand, they then apply for entrance to the Concordia Theological Seminary (CTSFW), Ft. Wayne, Indiana, for entrance to the master of divinity degree program or to Concordia Seminary, St. Louis, Missouri. The other path of becoming a pastor in the LCMS is what is called the Colloquy Program (a conversion to LCMS). For example, it might be possible for a Catholic priest or a Methodist minister to become a pastor in LCMS through the complexity of the Colloquy Program. Officially the applicant candidates can be (1) graduates not yet serving from other Christian denominations degree programs, (2) active pastors from other Christian church bodies, (3) licensed lay deacons from the LCMS with ten or more years of experience, or (4) licensed lay deacons that are required to apply by Resolution Convention of Synod 13-02A. There is also an alternative program that does not require a master's in divinity degree. The point here is one cannot feel the call to be a minister of the Gospel one day and become a pastor in an LCMS church the next day. It's an academically difficult path to trod, and that is a good thing. In spite of that we still experience a few bad apples but fortunately have a way to deal with that problem when it occurs. Having an easier path would be a disservice to the congregations, the tradition, and the work of the Reformation itself, not to mention serve to dilute the truth and the value of the Gospel message over time. The influence a pastor has on his congregational members cannot be overstated, and I for one prefer to have someone with the background, education, and temperament to succeed in gaining and maintaining Christ's flock on earth and on their path to heaven.

To find out more about the expectations we have for pastors and full-time church workers, look in your Bible and read Titus 1:5–9; 1 Timothy 3:2–7; Timothy 4:1–16; and 2 Timothy 4:1–5, again a high hurdle to cross over.

We can also count on a baseline education and additional screening of our pastors. Lutheran men called to be pastors do not need to deny their maleness for their vocation. Most pastors have a wife and a family and are able to relate to the same family issues you have to deal with—they have them too. They are not isolated from the realities of everyday life, from the community, from normal sexuality. Occasionally there are scandals involving Lutheran pastors; they too are normal sinful men. Yet my bet would be that if somebody counted, scandalous occurrences would be far fewer in the Lutheran churches.

REASON #60. Our pastors admit that they are sinners too and that they fall short of living a Godly life in full adherence to the law; only Jesus did that. If you have read 59, you will know that it takes a bit of grit and determination to become a pastor in the first place, but no amount of grit and determination is going to make pastors perfect or sinless in God's sight. They collectively and individually are sinners in their own right. Perhaps they feel worse about it when they sin, but sin they do, and the wise ones will admit it, might even quietly share what they are most tempted by. As parishioners we have high expectations of them for how they lead their lives, and that is not a bad thing as long as those expectations do not cross into the realm of expecting perfect and sinless behavior. Pastors have to struggle against the work of the devil and all earthly temptations just as we do. Some would say they are an even bigger target for the devil and his working toward evil. In my way of thinking, it takes a very special man and a high dose of fortitude to know that once you become ordained, all eyes are going to be on you with high expectations for near perfect behavior in all circumstances every second of the rest of your life. As pastors they have to admit it (sin); as congregational members we have to accept it and share in the grace of God with them that brought redemption and salvation to all penitent sinners, just like us.

REASON #61. It is OK to drink wine and beer and eat anything if we just stay within some level of moderation. Be strong enough to avoid the excesses is a core message in Lutheran circle. No one likes a drunk, and habitual drunks are extremely hard to love. We do not condone street drugs or pot (marijuana), any drugs that would bend your mind. Recreational drug use is an anathema to us. No street drugs, really. People laugh at my bubble gum allegory, but it might be true. I advise young parents to never let their children chew gum, ever, because it is a gateway to other bad things. I say I never met a smoker, pot-head, alcoholic, or druggie that did not chew gum first.

It is OK to drink wine. The biblical example from the Book of John tells of Jesus turning water into wine at a wedding feast as his more public life began. Martin Luther surely drank beer, as did all his contemporaries. Jesus canceled with his words the prohibitions on certain types of foods. It all boils down to exercising some discipline and taking into our bodies (God's dwelling place) these and all good things in moderation. A two-drink limit, eight ounces of pulled pork, or one serving of chocolate candy. Jesus said we are defiled by what comes out of our mouths, not by what goes into them to sustain our bodies and minds. It is a reverse endorsement of all healthy foods but an endorsement nonetheless. To Lutherans it's a license to eat whatever we please, whenever we please. It may not be good for our waistlines and meeting weight charts, but we know that our enemy is unbelief or unrepentantly breaking God's law, not food or lifestyle or wealth or poverty. There are no taboo foods for us: Pork is OK; being a vegan or vegetarian is OK; eating beef every day is OK. What we eat or do not eat is not part and parcel of our religion. We are free to enjoy in moderation all the foods harvested from the earth.

We can eat or drink any food because we are Christians and free to do so. We discipline our intake because we are free to respond to his love for us by keeping his dwelling place rational, sober, and healthy. In a scriptural and literal sense, our bodies are vessels for the Holy Spirit and our own souls and should be treated with the utmost respect.

REASON #62. We believe God came down to us, not the other way around. We see God as having come to earth to rescue us, not ourselves working our behavior or way of life to "rise" to heaven by doing good works, meditating, or denying ourselves. Religions that require you to lift yourself up to a deity are the opposite message to the principle at the core of Christian belief, that God took the action and sent his Son (the God-man), Jesus, to carry the burden of our sin, the sin of the whole world on his shoulders on the Cross of Calvary. There is no way that we, with our human frailties, can work (meditate, fast, sacrifice, perform good works, think, buy, reason, walk, chart the stars) hard enough to raise ourselves up to God and his heaven on our own. If we as mere humans could do that, join ourselves to heaven—no one would stay on planet earth. Our birth, life, salvation, earthly death, and passage to heaven are in his hands, not our own. The control freak in our flawed human nature does not want to accept that our salvation is not of our own doing, and that is why these other religions exist and still thrive after these few thousand years after Christ's appearance and preaching.

REASON #63. Typically our sermons only make us feel bad one or two times a year. Those days in the church calendar would be mostly Ash Wednesday and nearly always Good Friday. Some services I have attended in other churches have been real letdowns on the way out of the church service all year long, the down message being you will never measure up and there is no hope of you ever going to heaven unless you do x, y, and z, and then even after that, maybe not. The constant negative message about sinful us (men and women) weighs heavy on your heart and mind, and you begin to ask yourself, Why did I even come to this church and service and listen to this pastor anyway? Never a good feeling. If I were arrogant or ignorant enough to not know I was a sinner, I probably would not have walked through these church doors anyway.

The reverse message is, in my thought process, just as disheartening. A church and pastor that is always preaching a sugar high: Everything is peaches and cream with us and you because you're here today and we are so different from those people out there, we can rejoice in our salvation. Sorry about the rest of you, but we are going to be blessed and rich, and all our problems are going away if you are born again in our midst. Come on down to the altar to be born again if you are not sure. I find both extremes in content inappropriate and view them as harmful in both the short and long run to the faith, my faith, your faith. Some days in real life the peaches and cream become sour and rancid to the point of poison as the devil's work catches up with us. When the sugar high wears off, the feel-good preaching messages falls pretty flat at that point.

Going to a church to hear the depressing message week after week simply brings you as the congregant to despair and finds you looking for uplifting messages in places where you should not be going. Even then the "You are almost good enough" message lands hard; but then comes the "Stop by and do some good works" or "Send some money, and we'll see about that ticket to heaven someday." Unfortunately pastors and preachers, and priests and bishops or whatever we call them, do not take an oath to do no harm to the hearer. All too many may not even know enough to know their teachings are doing harm and are contrary to the Gospel.

With this in mind I am happy to go to my Lutheran church on Ash Wednesday service and on Good Friday service to learn again how bad I am, a sinner in every respect, and be reminded of the suffering and weight of sin Jesus took on himself to make salvation work for us sinners, one and all. I leave with a heavy heart on Ash Wednesday and am thankful for it because I get it, get what it took to get that ticket for me. I come back for Good Friday service, and that message is hammered a little deeper into my heart and soul, and again I leave with a heavy heart but with great anticipation of the coming Easter Sunday morning celebration when I am again reminded that Jesus triumphed over the devil and the grave, and paid the price for our redemption and return to God's Kingdom. These two days are days of the church and year calendar I would not trade away for anything. Grateful for those few days, emphasis on *few*, of serious condemnation.

We truly were stardust at one time, making the parts each of us is composed of as roughly 13.8 billion years old. First these parts were pure energy, then a gas, then particles, then atoms. The egg your mother made you from with a little help from your dad was there shortly after her own conception, tie us to the dust imposed on our foreheads on Ash Wednesday. "Remember that you are dust, and to dust you shall return" are the ancient words spoken on Ash Wednesday to remind us of our mortality and need for redemption.

REASON #64. We can own and carry guns and hunt and fish. Mostly we are a peaceful people, but we are not weak. Not too weak to live on a ranch and slaughter a pig, sheep, or beef cattle to make it become a part of our daily bread. We can hunt and fish and even hold a wild game dinner event as a fund-raiser for something for the church. We abhor wanton waste of those once-living wild resources or waste of any resources for that matter. Hunting or fishing for sport, supplementing our food stores, or hunting or fishing for survival is not a problem for Lutherans; doing so is one of the many things in this world you can freely engage in without affecting your salvation.

REASON #65. There is no big change from church to church as you travel. Service styles (traditional, high church, contemporary, modern) will vary from one Missouri Synod Lutheran to another as you travel; yet for the most part, you will be using one or more of the Lutheran service formats, liturgies, hymnals, or service supplements that are consistent with our expectations as Lutherans and in harmony with standards for worship expected by the synod. As with all generalizations, there will be exceptions, and I can only remember visiting one or two churches I would not go back to because the service was "off the chart" and not consistent with Lutheran doctrine and my expectations for the service to be conducted "decently and in order." During the worship service one comes to expect conviction of sin followed by an assurance of absolution, the Lord's Prayer, the Apostles' or Nicene Creed, a message consistent with New Testament teaching, and a hymn of praise at some point during the service, and when these elements are not present, it more than disappoints. There is in my opinion no point in going back to these off-beat churches for a second helping when this occurs.

REASON #66. We can salute the flag of our respective nations. Jesus was asked in the New Testament as reported in the Book of Matthew, Chapter 22, about whether it was within the laws of God to pay taxes to the Roman government controlling Israel at the time. His reply, paraphrased, was "to render to Caesar that which is Caesar's and to God that which is his." Worldwide, Lutherans and other Christians recognize that the geographic governments to which we are subjugated do not and should not change our relationship to God. Saluting the flag, paying taxes, and obeying the just laws of our respective nations such as the United States of America will not keep us out of heaven or deny us the ability to daily pursue a Godlier, more God-fearing and God-respecting life. Beware of any religion that presupposes that the government of your land and the religion of those in a majority or minority in your land become one or become combined in any way. It is said this way: The government you are under is God's left hand; the church you are a participant in is God's right hand at work in your life and the world. Both are necessary for a peaceful and tranquil civic space where we can all freely live out our lifelong walk with God. This wisdom of render to Caesar and to God is one of many pieces of wisdom expressed by Jesus that became one of the bedrocks of our American civic principles.

REASON #67. There are nine LCMS-affiliated Lutheran colleges and universities. They are located in Bronxville, New York; Mequon, Wisconsin; Ann Arbor, Michigan; Seward, Nebraska; Austin, Texas; St. Paul, Minnesota; Forest River, Illinois; Portland, Oregon; and Irvine, California. From these educational institutions the synods' churches benefit with a supply of full-time church workers, music directors, and parochial school teachers. These institutions are often a feeder path for men called to the ministry to attend one of our two seminaries. Our pastoral seminaries are located in St. Louis, Missouri, and Ft. Wayne, Indiana. The availability of a Lutheran/Christian-based education system is a blessing to the church and the products of those institution become a blessing to the world.

REASON #68. The quickest and quirkiest description of our faith is "Catholic without the Guilt." This is the one description my wife, a former Catholic, uses particularly when speaking about her religion with her still Catholic friends and acquaintances. After having attended a number of Catholic services over the course of my life, I can easily notice the similarities in the conduct of the service. The pattern of the homily or sermon can even closely parallel those I have regularly heard in the Lutheran Church. The hope of salvation is presented, that we can all be saved through the undeserved grace of God's gift in the gift of our Savior Jesus Christ. The difference between the two religions that I've noticed is that in a Catholic service before the end of the preaching, you are left to think that only "maybe you are saved" if only you measure up in some way or another. That is not to say we should not cooperate when God extends his hand in grace to us. In one example, Penny and I attended a Catholic service with some of her relatives where the priest was a convert from another Christian religion and had been married when he converted to Catholicism. During his sermon, I was tracking right with him and remember thinking to myself about 15 minutes into his homily that "Wow, if this is the Catholic Church now, I could attend." Well, in the next 5 minutes I again felt "Wow," but this time I thought, "Lucky to Be Lutheran," because in the last 5 minutes he piled on the guilt again. The guilt is always there, putting the brakes on messages that could otherwise be totally uplifting. Catholics too can be saved, no question, God bless them. But for me, I much prefer to leave the guilt in the first half of the service, which happens with most of the Lutheran services. Notable exceptions can be Ash Wednesday, occasionally Maundy Thursday, and Good Friday; the Lutheran pastors seem to do their best to make you feel bad about yourself as you exit the service on at least one of those days. Sometimes you need that. Most times you don't.

REASON #69. The reluctant founder of our version of the Christian faith was wise, learned almost in a divine way, yet a colorful sinner just like us. A rebel with a cause was Martin Luther as we see him through the lens of history, his cause to return to the original truths of the Gospel message. It seems that, with the passage of time and human influences, we find that negative substance through people who are in influential positions tend to corrupt core values in every type of organization. The budding universal church, which we now call the Catholic Church, evolved in its understanding and teachings for over 1,500 years before Martin pounded a few nails and posted a list of some thoughts to debate with the church hierarchy on October 31, 1517. During that first 1,500 years, some of the simplicity, truth, and power of that original Gospel message was corrupted and lost to the church. Fast-forward another 501 years, and that core value understanding was diluted again through the actions of men replacing God's core message with their own thoughts. Essentially the downside of the Reformation was that it made splitting off seem like the thing to do, resulting in, as noted in the previous sentence, a diluted core message. By using the term "diluted," I am referring to the fact that there are about 40 Lutheran church bodies in the United States and about another 40 nonoperational Lutheran synods that have since ceased to exist. When you add in the fact that there may be as many as 50,000 other Protestant denominations worldwide, the term "diluted" may not do justice to what is happening to the unadulterated Gospel message that Luther was attempting to return to. You can clearly see the influence of sin here, or we would all be on the same page with our doctrine and beliefs.

Think about this for a moment: Your understanding of a point or piece of information is in your head. Your limited ability to transfer that understanding is through a touch, a smell, a graphic, a sound, speech, and the written word. Even with those communication tools, a point does not always cross from one person to another with the same meaning with which it was sent. With this in mind, recall that there were only 12 disciples at first as conveyors of the Gospel from Jesus's lips to them and from them to the masses they brought into the faith during the infancy of the faith in those early years. So, even if the original 12 disciples all had a slightly different understanding of the faith, nuanced in some way by their unique experience and intellect, one would expect no more than 12 versions of Christian doctrine and beliefs to exist today. It is nothing more or less than stunning and frightening at the same time that so many versions do exist today. This is why we in the LCMS pray for what we call the "unity of doctrine." On the one hand, diversity of preaching may reach people of different mindsets or backgrounds; on the other hand, the various doctrines cannot all be right, and the wrongheaded preaching is leading people astray. Sometimes to very bad places and poison soup, literally and figuratively. False prophets are very much alive today, on satellite, TV, radio, the web, and blogs. Without some training and knowledge of the Bible, and even with some, it is easy to be led to trust in falsehoods.

In April 1847 the German Evangelical Lutheran Synod of Missouri, Ohio and Other States was founded and later became LCMS. And for the next 171 years, the little squabbles and debates have raged on about what it means to be a Lutheran Christian and what we should believe, teach, and confess. I have seen the drift over my own lifetime (which is a small blip in time) of the movement to a more social, less biblical set of principles being used to govern the churches in some quarters of the country. The happy part is that LCMS is moving less, slower to change, which is good, because no one can find salvation in an empty vessel or in watered-down teaching. Too much change and LCMS too will die as a synod. Again, we may need a reluctant, wise, learned, and colorful sinner to pull us all back to that core message of the Gospel. I'd like to think that the Missouri Synod is still the closest to getting most all doctrinal issues correct.

REASON #70. Congregations have the power and responsibility to select their own pastors. Luther suggested to his followers who were bringing about new congregations during his lifetime to select pastors from their midst from within the congregation of believers by a vote of the congregation and not by appointment of a bishop. Today we say "called." The process has been hijacked by some regional district presidents who attempt to manipulate the process a bit too much. It should go something like this, barring outside influence: The congregation in need requests a "call list" from the district, which is supposed to provide names of pastors who feel the need to make a change for some reason or new graduates who have not yet been placed. Once this list is received, the congregation shares the list at a church voters' meeting and also asks for nominations from the floor from those present. A call committee is appointed. It draws up the offer and call specifications defining what the congregation is looking for and prepares more information about all the candidates including those nominated from the floor. This information is shared with the congregation, and another voters' meeting is held to select by vote a top-three list of people to call for a visit and interviews. Some pastors may pass outright and not interview. Once the interview is over, the congregation votes on its selection—the hope is, with a unanimous vote of the voters assembled. That pastor then receives the call. If he accepts, he is installed as pastor there. The process is not perfect, but the hand of God is acting within the process by moving the congregation to vote for a particular candidate and for the candidate to feel that his acceptance of the call is God's will. When a pastor selected through this process declines, here is where the members of the local church leadership can fail. They should insist on a new call list from the district with 100 percent new names of candidates and then begin the whole process over. When you see an unselected name appear on a list a second time, that is potentially district meddling trying to control the process. Ultimately it is the congregation's responsibility to act in a way that is expressing God's will and not the district president's preference. Again, strong leadership is the key for a local congregation to ensure an impartial, unbiased process open to God working his will for that congregation. The bottom line is that district presidents do not always know best, and it is the congregation's call to make.

REASON #71. Some LCMS districts run regional Christian-oriented summer camps. Opportunities for camp youth programs exist, and many churches run a few days or a week or two of Vacation Bible School sessions for youth from the church and their friends from the neighborhood. This is excellent that these events occur; however, their presence and availability is not necessarily sufficient to make up for the 1977 demise of the Walther League for middle grade and high school youth. Youth events and clubs at the local parish do work out in some local churches; yet overall the nurturing and mentoring of youth in the truths of the Gospel is an area that certainly needs more work and focus from congregations, districts, and synod levels.

REASON #72. Many of our churches have a nursery. No one really minds having small children in the church service. They can be sweet, adorable, and even amusing when things are going well for them. When that is not the case for children and things are getting challenging, it is nice for parents to be able to go to another space with a speaker system to quiet and attend to their child and still be able to hear the sermon and service. Some churches also have accommodations for mothers who are nursing their babies. Children of all ages are always welcome in the service though, and it is a good thing to bring them to the service. Some pastors will have set aside time for a children's message that is in some way, it is hoped, tied into the Gospel message for that day. A rare practice I do not favor is when, as a part of the structure of the Sunday service time, children are separated from the assembly and go to another area in the church for a children's service or message. As a parent I would not have attended a church with this practice for two reasons: I want to know what my children are being taught or told without giving up my own service attendance to do it, and I want my children and spouse in church with me as the expected act of a family at worship together. To me that is the normal expectation as God intended it to be, families gathered together in worship. We are all his children.

REASON #73. Lutherans are serious about the worship music and the instruments that make it. Pipe organs and trained organists are our stock in trade on Sunday morning for the older churches that are blessed to still have both. Not sure if electronic organs or stringed pianos would take first or second place. The traditional hymns in use in most all of our congregations were written and annotated for natural instrumentation: reed organs, trumpets, pipe organs, harps, clarinets, and the like. A minority of our churches use electric guitars, drums, and digital keyboards during all or some of their services in an attempt to be modern or more contemporary, and minimize the use of the traditional tunes and lyrics from the hymn books. This use of contemporary music is done as an attempt to "appeal to younger people" in the belief it will lead to church growth. Not entirely sure it works or if it is a good idea to abandon the strong and reinforcing religious lessons and messages contained in the traditional hymns. Clearly what matters most is the delivery of the complete law and Gospel message from the pulpit. Music plays a secondary supportive role and very important buttressing of the sermon message whether it is contemporary or traditional.

One church I attended was extraordinary in that it had two pipe organs, one in the front of the church and one in the back of the church. Parts of the front organ were wired to the keyboard in the rear balcony of the church. Occasionally at this church two organists were deployed during the services to present the full richness of sound that only could come from the use of both pipe organs. The organists at this church were highly accomplished, and the music was always excellent and uplifting.

REASON #74. We can enjoy music, beautiful art, and dance outside the church. Even those not able to dance would be permitted to if they could. We do not have to deny ourselves a normal life because our "church" inappropriately publishes and applies rules like "Don't dance" (although at times in our history dance has been discouraged), "Avoid museums," "Don't cut your hair" if you are a woman, or "Don't wear jewelry," just to name a few of the taboos I have heard other denominations have.

As a Lutheran you are supposed to be a "light to the world," an everyday example of virtuous living. The reason to live a Godly life as an example to the world around you is to not cause others to move away from the Gospel message by using you as their "bad" example. If you as a Lutheran Christian are a bad example through living a sin-filled life, why would others want to embrace Christianity? To the outside world you appear as a hypocrite professing a Christian life in church on Sunday and then living as a sinner on Monday, breaking God's laws and commandments. However, appreciating music, enjoying works of art, wearing jewelry, or dancing the tango is not a sin; quite the contrary, appreciating what God has equipped us to do mirrors the magnificence of his creation.

REASON #75. LCMS through Concordia publishes a directory of all our churches, pastors, and church workers. The directory is called *The Lutheran Annual* (by year). This is one of my favorite "travel" directories, as it makes it really easy to find a church compatible with my comfort zone and beliefs when I am out of town. I can learn the pastor's name from the directory and ask for him by name when we wish to visit and partake in Holy Communion while traveling. The seminary that the pastor graduated from is also listed. Sections of the annual include "Organizations, Officers, and Structure"; "Congregations"; "Ordained Ministers"; "Commissioned Ministers"; "Schools"; "Ministries: General Information (statistics)"; and an index. This book takes all the guesswork out of finding a church when one is traveling and provides much other information of interest. In one handy volume the contact information is there for one's easy use.

REASON #76. We are saints on both sides of the curtain of death.
Perhaps for some who have been brought up in or are familiar with other Christian denominations, the concept of we earthly sinners being saints may be both hard to grasp and perhaps even hard to accept. Yet saints we are, only in that like any of the famous historical saints of the church, we too are washed by Jesus's sacrifice and his shed blood and share in the promised inheritance just like the saints of old. We do not accept the work righteous views that life, your life, has to reach some standard here on earth to get into heaven; we do not believe that you have to work your way with good deeds and stay as sinless as possible so that you might get to heaven with the saints someday and be one yourself. Once we have accepted as truth the promise of the Gospel that Jesus was the propitiation for all our sins (and indeed the sins of all mankind, past, present, and future) as a repentant soul sorry for our sins, we become saints. We stay saints even when we commit that next sin, repent again, and trust that God will continue to work his way in our hearts. Anyone who rejects that core message of the Gospel is doomed to a life now and a life in eternity without God. That, being without God, is hell here now and after death.

REASON #77. The "church year" follows the changes of the four seasons. We start the year with Advent, followed by the Christmas Season, next Epiphany Season, then the Lenten Season, Holy Week leading up to Easter Season, and finally the Time of the Church (either Pentecost or Holy Trinity) to complete the church year. There are details and special Sundays to fill in under those major divisions of the year—much like how on a secular basis we notice the comings and goings of the four seasons in weather. These changes coincidently seem to complement each other as the year progresses. Mostly besides looking at the secular calendar for the year where religious holidays are mentioned, we also notice that the altar covers (paraments) and the pastoral stoles will change color to make note of and amplify the changing focus of the various dedicated Sundays throughout the church worship year. Throughout the year some feasts and festivals are celebrated, some as commemorations of persons or events that played a role in the development of a uniform delivery of the Gospel over time.

This calendar-driven practice and focus provides a connection to the past, provides a remembrance of some ideals, and causes us to focus on what the church has both achieved and endured over time. This varied service focus and schedule connects us as worshipers to the flow of time both historically and in our own lives. With this worship calendar taking us receptively through the church year(s), we mark out the years before our eventual reunion in heaven with all the saints who have gone before us, getting ever closer to joining them in celebrations and victory over the devil and his works and our own sin.

REASON #78. We have no prohibited clothing or required manner of dress. I won't quite say that anything goes when attending church or living your daily life as a Lutheran. But we are not like some denominations where your manner of grooming and style of dress matter, or there are prohibited or required forms of dress. We take the focus off our earthly outward appearance and instead count on the cloak of Jesus to make us appear clean and "in white robes" before God. We can wear jewelry and have facial hair, beard or moustache, or not. Women can wear a head covering in church if they choose to or not. Women can have long hair, cut their hair short, or wear hats or not. Not to say that modesty does not matter, but pretty much any outfit that you would wear to an office or restaurant and that is not destined to malfunction would be OK, again assuming some modesty is apparent in the choice. What is acceptable or at least tolerated has come a long way from the days of my youth where hats, "Sunday best" dresses, and white gloves were not uncommon as churchgoing attire. This ability, this privilege, to make our own choices comes under the heading of "Christian freedom" and should therefore as a privilege not be abused. The point is, we are free to choose, within good taste and reason, and there are no edicts from the pulpit or our doctrine about our dress or adornments. For those of us who think blue jeans with a dress belt is dressed up and blue jeans with a cowboy buckle is casual, we are good to go to church either way.

REASON #79. I can be fully in and live in the real world without being a product of the world. Our lives as Lutherans are not much different from that of our neighbors and friends, our fellow citizens. We drink beer at home; go to movies of all rating stripes; watch and participate in sports, NASCAR included; stop by the pub on occasion for a cocktail and plate of burgers or fish and fries. We Lutherans live pretty normal lives just like everyone else. The big difference may be that it is not our purpose; our purpose-goal-intention is to be children of God, essentially citizens of heaven during our exiled life on earth, and when we pass through the curtain of death, we are simply coming home. Separating ourselves from society or living a monastic lifestyle not necessary. In fact, we can do good by being in the world when our lives, speech, and moral principles become positive examples to the unchurched. In a salt-of-the-earth sort of way, we can be sharing the flavor of a Christian, God-fearing, God-respecting lifestyle with our neighbors.

REASON #80. We get the most important points of the Gospel contained in the Bible covered in Sunday services in either one or three years. Pastors choose either the one-year or three-year lectionary readings for the Sunday church services. Following a pattern from week to week in the church services throughout the year is a Christian practice that dates back to A.D. 300 to 400, perhaps earlier. The three-year plan, currently the most popular in churches for reading the key Gospel texts, starts with Matthew texts in year 1, Mark in year 2, and Luke in year 3. The more traditional one-year cycle is a parsed-down version that also covers important texts but repeats every year. There are a lot of benefits that accrue to the congregation in either plan: The most obvious is that the sermons are supposed to reflect some amplification of some point or points in the Gospel lesson. If nothing else, following either lectionary schedule achieves some variety in the service and sermons. Would hate to have to listen to a one-show pony every week. Our triune God—Father, Son, and Holy Spirt—and God's plan to redeem us is a lot more interesting, making following the lectionary (either one) like turning the pages in a riveting book from week to week.

REASON #81. We are reassured every week of our salvation. Well almost. Color me disappointed if I sit through a sermon in an LSMS church conducted by a called and ordained pastor where I do not hear somewhere along the way during the sermon the points of conviction, repentance, and salvation through Jesus as Savior through the grace of God. So different from other churches I have attended where the core message was "You're almost good enough to get to heaven" or "If you do enough good, you will be in heaven," or where I heard a lesson on some humanistic lesson or endeavor. Worse yet, at least for me, are the church sermons that require "altar calls" in order to be saved this week, or tell you if you love God enough, he will make you rich. Don't need or want some feel-good contrived bunk sermon ever. If being reminded that God loved us enough and sent his Son, Jesus (God and man), to save you is not enough to make you feel good every minute of every day of your life, then no hyped-up "kum ba yah" sermon will help you, certainly not for long. When the real adversities we all suffer at some time in this life catch up with us, there is nothing that will help. Also disappointed with preaching that leaves you or me thinking, "Well that's nice, but now what?" Meaning any sermon message that left off the salvation part. That is why I am so thankful that most every Sunday when the sermon sings out in my LCMS church, it is on point with the lessons of the Gospel message and leaves me disappointed on the rare occasions when it is not included.

REASON #82. Most all of our Lutheran beliefs are succinctly articulated and codified in the three creeds we recite. The Apostles' Creed, the Nicene Creed, and the Athanasian Creed and in our daily plead in the Lord's Prayer. We are to pray to God in all three person-ages of the Father, Son, and Holy Spirit from examples of doing so that are found in many places in the Bible. We pray these prayers for a lot of reasons, not the least of which is that we are told to pray in the second of the Ten Commandments. Praying these prayers reminds us of the completeness, strength, and yet the simplicity of the Gospel message. In simple terms, pray, praise, and give thanks to God in your prayer life inside and outside the church building. Doing so strengthens your faith.

REASON #83. Church-run elementary and high schools are available in many places. Church-sponsored day care, primary schools, and in some places high schools are available should you choose to have your children educated in an environment that respects your Christian religious beliefs. These schools charge tuition for financial support, and congregations often add money to support, operate, and maintain the schools. The number of these schools appears to be dropping, as couples have fewer children and congregations are "graying." There is also competition in many states from academy schools that are able to get state or federal financial support but purport to offer a higher-quality education. Any recognition that God exists and teaching of common sense both seem to be totally lacking in public education in most places, so it is regrettable there are not more Lutheran-run schools. Forty-seven states have either or both early childhood and elementary Lutheran schools, and twenty-nine states have either or both junior high and high schools. Parents where these schools are available have to make the choice of placing their children in these schools where God is not left totally out of the curriculum. These days it appears to me that if your children are not in a Lutheran school, as a parent you should ensure they are in Sunday school classes until they graduate from high school, just as a defensive measure for your children's souls if for no other reason.

REASON #84. There is no purgatory on the path to heaven. This relates to one of the many root causes of the Reformation and Luther's posting on the door at Wittenberg that changed world history and church history. It is hard to get theological agreement on purgatory being a stopover on the path to heaven—about when you go to heaven—because of one chapter in the Bible that talks about the resurrection to come, Jesus's second coming, a coming rapture, you name it. Here is how I look at it after a lifetime of sitting in the pew in Lutheran churches and listening to the sermons. No one can deny when Jesus, from the cross, looked over at one being crucified with him and said, to paraphrase a bit, "Today you will be with me in paradise." There is no purgatory unless you want to count your time on earth as a purgatory of sorts. There is no Jesus saying. "You are going into the ground like everybody else, and for a few hundred millennia your soul will sleep. Then I will come and wake you up from the ground and take you to my Father's, your Father's, house in heaven." You have a soul. It, your soul, has energy and mass. And when you die, your soul leaves your body (this can be measured scientifically) on its way to meet your maker; or for those who have rejected God's grace in the Gospel, your soul goes straight to hell. It is that simple.

Now this transition from life to earthly death happens fairly quickly. You feel a mild pain for a moment as your soul's essence is ripped from your earthly body, and then you feel no pain and peace. Then you (your soul, what makes you you) passes through a starry-filled tunnel to the light. At that point, someone you will recognize from your family or family of believers meets you and greets you just before you get to cross the threshold to heaven to see Jesus. If your work on earth is not done, you are sent back; if it is done and you get through the proverbial pearly gates, there and then you will meet Jesus and be with him, **God** the Father, and the Holy Spirit, who has been with you all your life, providing that connection between your soul and your heart all your life. The angel choirs will be there and the whole community of believers who have passed on before you. As a believer you will ask at the door of heaven to "see Jesus" by saying "I want to go inside to see Jesus," perhaps more than once.

Your personal gatekeeper will let you pass and go in with you if it is indeed your time. Others will be told by the gatekeeper that Jesus is not ready to see you yet and that you have to go back now, as there is work to be done by you, but not to worry; Jesus will be here when your time arrives. Those souls that are "sent back," who have more work to do for the Kingdom, they will feel abandoned for a moment as their souls are falling to earth to be reunited with their earthly body. On the way back they see their clinically dead body lying there from a few feet above for a moment and then no more when they feel excruciating pain and an electric shock for an instant when their heart instantly starts to beat again and breathing resumes, first with difficulty, then with ease. You cannot see Jesus until your work for the Kingdom here on earth is done. Don't ask me how I know this is the process; just trust that I do. Even some faithful believers will doubt this progression, and so will some pastors; and atheists will say it's the brain being starved, and still others will make something up about why this is unbelievable. The reality is that for some folks, sadly, the truth is sometimes hard to accept until you personally experience that truth, and everyone who is reading this book will clinically die someday, some only once; some more than once. At the point of your own death, you can do a fact check on my accounting of the process; until then, believers will accept that is the way it goes and will find themselves as souls in heaven with God eternally, and unbelievers will be arriving in the depths of hell and despair separated from God for all eternity.

Now from time to time, you will hear theologians talking about the levels of heaven or rooms in God's mansion; they will talk about being reunited with a recognizable form of your earthly grave dust, skin, and bones on Judgment Day, and you will hear other religious scholars talk about glorified bodies, maybe just like the one Jesus used when he walked through closed doors and walls after his own resurrection from the dead. Those discussions are interesting, and they may even be correct; who knows for sure if any of those thoughts about how it is to live the life with God in heaven forever will come to pass as theologians describe it? It makes for good conversation for those of sufficient faith to engage in the topics. My advice, however, is to be entirely concerned about your own soul, not the form it will have; instead focus on accepting the message of the Gospel, that Jesus paid the price for entry to heaven for everyone who does not deny him. Leave the rest of the details up to God as he has already got it all figured out for you.

REASON #85. There is no promise of being joined to "celestial" beings on the other side for us if we die for the faith. The concept of Christian martyrdom does not escape us with heaven as its ultimate reward; however, we are not called on, or enticed, or encouraged to sacrifice our lives in that way. Even though martyrdom came to many in the Christian faith in the past, is still happening today, and could happen to any believers by circumstances not of their own making in the future. Our concept of heaven does not relate to sex as a reward; it relates to being joyful, happy, content in the very presence of God and with all believers (saints) for all eternity. As our country, and the world really, is becoming more occupied by people of no faith, no religion at all, and other religions whose beliefs and practices are not in concert with Holy Scripture, there is no more important Lutheran organization at work today than POBLO International, headquartered in Clinton Township, Michigan. POBLO's stated mission goal is "To meet the physical, social, and spiritual needs of Muslims and other immigrants and refugees in the United States by sharing the love of Jesus in practical and culturally relevant ways" (quoted from its webpage at http://www.poblo.org). I personally have a great deal of respect and admiration for all the people who work in and volunteer for this Christian outreach right here at home along with those who support it with donations.

REASON #86. We have as outreach auxiliaries the Lutheran Laymen's League (LLL) and Lutheran Women's Missionary League (LWML). Most churches of the LCMS will have local chapters of LWML, individually managed within the congregation. Each chapter is made up of a few locally elected or selected leaders who will keep in touch with the national office and district-level operatives to maintain the programs and outreach objectives of the group. It is the fully sanctioned women's group of the LCMS. The Lutheran Women's Missionary League works to encourage and prepare women of all ages to live out their Christian lives and to be active in mission projects and events to support local to global missions. To find out more about LWML, visit http://www.lwml.org/who-we-are.

Lutheran Laymen's League is the official men's (now women's too) organization of the LCMS. The Lutheran Laymen's League governs and supports the Lutheran Hour Ministries, a Christian outreach that bills itself as ministry empowering and equipping churches to communicate the Gospel to all people. To find out more about LLL, visit https://www.lhm.org/about/. It is not as high profile as the LWML, and not every church can boast an active chapter.

As an "old" or "new" Lutheran, you'll find that both of these organizations and a lot of local churches' one-off clubs or groups are a good place to start doing more for the furtherance of the Gospel message and enjoying some good fellowship at the same time.

REASON #87. Some pastors dislike going to the district conventions as much as the lay delegates do. Not sure of all the reasons for this, because this is how our collective churches influence and set policy to run the synod. There are others, both lay and pastoral delegates, who look forward to them and delight in being a part of the gathering and process. This is where operational, management, and doctrinal issues are discussed and voted on to advance a proposal or question on to the national convention. Both district and national conventions are held in alternate years every three years (district held in even years, national in odd). I think a lot of the pushback is relevant, beyond "We just don't like change," because our doctrine is not broken and there is no need to tweak it very much. The districts and the synod officers and offices are functioning, so why change anything? That is often the question asked. For the most part the work is getting done, and the affiliated organizations are doing their work every day, so if it isn't broken, why fix it? From my own experience attending a district convention, there was a lot of worship, fellowship, and good food—and aside from that a lot of talking and very few initiatives that were advanced. When I went home after the weeks' worth of convention, I was all OK with the lack of change for the sake of change. Since the Bible and the Lutheran confessions have worked for a very long time now, what is worth altering? Perhaps one thing, however: The synod over the years has painted itself and us into a corner over the one thing that could be changed, that perhaps should be taught in a different manner that would allow hundreds, thousands, even tens of thousands of new people to embrace the Lutheran (Christian) faith without hints of intellectual compromise.

REASON #88. We are not a feel-good or "God will make you rich" church. Nor do we say "Send your money to God, but please use our address." Our pastors live modest to upper-middle-class lives and are typically compensated comparatively or equivalent with the local communities' public school teachers with a master's degree as the minimum benchmark. The church congregations prepare a budget that includes a total compensation package for the pastors that in larger congregations can be over $100,000. We do not believe they should be tentmakers and pay their own way or should be turned into beggars for the sake of the Gospel. They are for the most part adequately compensated for the work they do, and it is not the intent of any LCMS congregation I know of to focus on "what the pastor can bring in." You will likely only hear sermons on stewardship or giving money to the church but once a year, unless the congregation faces financial difficulties. You are totally unlikely to hear a sermon preached that says give money to God here in our collection plate and when you go back to your business on Monday God will help make you rich.

REASON #89. The business functions of our Lutheran churches are run locally by an elected slate of officers and leaders. These elected positions form the "church council," and the church council is directed by the laypeople who are "voters" in the church and attend the voters' meetings. Voters are usually adults, but are at least confirmed members who have signed that particular congregation's constitution. The key elected roles of president, vice-president, secretary, financial secretary, and treasurer may vary from one congregation to another, but the key is that these are elected officials and have the legal responsibility for the secular affairs of the congregation as if it were a corporation. The spiritual life of the congregation is a team effort between the pastor and the elders of the church.

Various other boards and committees may be empowered to perform other work within the congregation and the community with proper oversight by the elected positions. Anything involving spiritual outreach to the community is overseen by the called pastor.

One folly of many smaller congregations is having too many elected and appointed positions to fill. It takes a Sunday attendance of upward of 150 to fill even the basic positions required for an efficient and effective church leadership. There is a huge difference in performance when someone actually enjoys doing the work over someone who "got stuck with it" because no one else would take the job. Church councils and voters in Lutheran churches have the power of the vote, and that vote can alter constitutional bylaws to add or eliminate positions covered in or authorized by the constitutional bylaws of the congregation.

It is OK in a smaller congregation to just be sure that Sunday or weekly services happen and the Good News of the Gospel is preached from the pulpit and taught in the children's Sunday school and in confirmation classes. For the average churchgoer, bigger or busier is not always better, and bells and whistles are not always required.

At times a church council will be faced with the ugly proposition that a pastor needs to be dismissed. Removal from any of the called-by-God positions in the church leadership such as pastor requires a council that is well grounded in biblical understanding and Lutheran traditions regarding a "your-fired" situation. There are two primary reasons this would be undertaken: a pastor who persistently teaches and preaches false doctrine and one who leads a very immoral life. That "immoral life" definition would include drug use, drunkenness, indecent liberties, and sexual assault. A secondary but no less important reason for removal would be the inability or refusal to perform the duties of his office. Even though the regional district office and district president have no vote in the matter of a congregation giving its pastor the boot to the curb, they are consulted and do get involved. Another reason a pastor may deserve the curb is by trying to control or actually being an overly controlling person in the financial business of the congregation or in the lives of the congregants.

It was no coincidence that Martin Luther, our first "Lutheran pastor," was a student of rhetoric and logic first on his intended path to become a lawyer before becoming a theologian. The twists and turns of the earthly church needed some straightening out. God set in motion the events that would bring him to be a man of the cloth with all the right learning and temperament to set his church back on a path more in tune with God's intent for the church. Whenever a pastor leaves that path, the local congregation has the responsibility to set things right.

REASON #90. **They will let you back or stay in the church even if you remarry after you experience a divorce.** The premise when young couples marry in the Lutheran Church is that they will stay together as husband and wife until one or both are dead. For many couples, reality strikes; and for both good and bad excuses or reasons, Lutherans do get divorced. Lutheran teaching is that infidelity on the part of one or the other of the couple is grounds for a divorce, where no reconciliation is possible. Human frailties being what they are and the realities of relationships, there are many other reasons that couples, or one person of the couple, find it necessary to divorce. One can think of those circumstances where divorce becomes a much more acceptable alternative—for example, to committing murder-suicide or tolerating being victimized by domestic violence. A divorce does not automatically become a reason for excommunication from the congregation although it can happen, though rarely, with some pastors and church councils and elders. To disallow members of the church to return who are divorced for whatever reason discounts the potential for true repentance, and before God there is forgiveness regardless of the severity of the sin. No Lutheran pastor that I ever met will ever say it is OK to get a divorce except for a spouse being unfaithful to the marriage vows and perhaps for abandonment by one spouse or for domestic abuse. Pastors do recognize that divorce happens to Lutherans and that we are all sinful and in need of redemption from all color of sin. Denying repentant reentry into the fellowship for divorced people or remarried couples is denying the power of God to forgive and repudiating equal application of the message and purpose of the Gospel message, that Christ died for all sin, all sinners. Suffice to say that Lutheran laity do have to observe or adhere to a principle of one wife or one husband at a time.

There is also not a lot of (or perhaps not any) support from pastors in the Lutheran faith for condoning "living together in sin, without the blessings of holy matrimony," even when it comes into play for the more senior among us, say ages of late 70s or 80s or even 90s where companionship and financial and enhanced mutual security are often the primary or only "friend" benefits of cohabitation. There are no verses in the Bible that call out, at least in my recollection, any topic specifically about cohabitation among seniors. In the family cultures of ages past, families would bother to care for their aging parents and grandparents, which is not necessarily the trend today. It would be hard to call all these senior men and women living together sinful if the participants are abstaining from sexual immorality; still, the assumption is often made that sin is present in these cohabitation-for-convenience relationships and excommunication occurs. The appearance of public immorality is apparently viewed as sinful as the actual immorality itself. In light of the door staying open to remarriage in Lutheran practice, perhaps seniors in these circumstances should consider to marry, if only for the convenience of social acceptance.

REASON #91. We do not join cults, societies, or fraternities with elements of religions in their beliefs and practices. Elks Lodge, Fraternal Order of the Eagles, Moose International, and the Masonic Lodge (Freemasonry) are all examples of organizations that have elements of religion within their practices that are contrary to biblical teaching and contrary to our doctrine as defined in the Book of Concord. Therefore, we are denied the endorsement or blessing of the church to be members of them due to the practices of these organizations that are contrary to Holy Scripture. Personally, even without the flawed beliefs and cult-like practices, regardless of the good they might do in society, any organization that asks you to take an oath, requires you to pay dues to "buy" your memberships or your friends, or has a "grand" anything, I personally want no part of. There are plenty of LCMS Recognized Service Organizations, 189 of them at this writing, that will provide an avenue to do good and help our fellow man. To find the list of these organizations and for more information, visit www.lcms.org/how-we-serve/mercy/recognized-service-organizations/directory. Aside from this list, most of our churches in North America and around the world have plenty of ways we can participate by being helping hands, strong backs, and wallets doing our Savior's work locally, statewide, nationally, and on the world stage.

REASON #92. There is a formal path and education system leading to a lay ministry position. Anyone can preach the word of God, share the message of salvation with family, friends, and strangers; one does not have to be a called and ordained minister to do that service in advancing the Kingdom. One does need to be educated, called, and ordained to be in the role of the pastoral office in the Missouri Synod churches. These roles reserved for called and ordained pastors include absolving sin, doing formal preaching, and presiding over the sacraments and in particular that of Holy Communion. Many laypeople feel the call to serve the church as a lifetime/full-time vocation, and the church recognizes this by making available formal education programs to properly equip them for various roles within the church. I know of a person that is well past age 65 who will be graduating from our St. Louis Seminary in the spring of 2019, so it is never too late to choose to serve.

REASON #93. We can do any calling for our life's work and live our life to the fullest. Some Lutherans as they come of age feel the call to work full time in the furtherance of God's Kingdom on earth and become pastors, teachers, and full-time church workers of many callings. The rest of us are equally responsible to further the Kingdom of God here on this earth, and yet we can choose any occupation from scavenger or trash collector to heart surgeon. It matters not what we do; it matters how we do it, which is to do it to the best of our ability and to honor God. Personally, I have been a garage mechanic and wrecker driver; bread truck delivery driver; sailor in the U,S. Navy; loan office assistant manager; Navy recruiter; life, health, and disability insurance agent; company expeditor; electrician; unemployed; U.S. Army and Michigan National Guard engineer officer; facilities management specialist; network engineer; information technology specialist; maintenance superintendent; work camper; elected village trustee; technology consultant; full-time retiree; salesman; and real property specialist. Oh, and let's not leave out writer and author. In all those work roles, I have never lost sight of the fact that this daily toil was and is to benefit my fellow man, support my family, and serve my God. In every case in every workplace, I was given opportunities to help others, advise others, serve others in some way. There were days along the way to show—to demonstrate in tangible and in intangible ways—God's love for us. At times there were opportunities to witness directly and to share a little bit of my faith in the Gospel message to others. In nearly every instance I was the guy that was happy to be there and happy to help others. This is, I believe, what God wants all of us to do no matter what we are doing for a living. I think this is what the LCMS teaches as well; if there were contrary messages on Sunday morning, I probably would have noticed.

Our work life is less than half of our waking hours, so what in the shadow of the cross of Calvary do we do with the rest of our time? We live our lives spending time with our family, neighbors, friends, and acquaintances and sometimes in the solitude of our own company. We live our lives to the fullest (because we only get one); we laugh, cry, serve, receive, recreate, volunteer, learn, teach. And whatever it is that we do, we do it knowing fully that Christ died for our sins, that we as repentant sinners by the grace of God share in the inheritance brought about by Jesus's redemptive work. There is no commandment that says we cannot have fun, compete, enjoy another's companionship, hunt, fish, play ball, travel, whatever it is that strikes our fancy or daring. God is with us no matter how we live life; we simply must remember also that we are with him and not cross the line with premeditated sins. While we live our lives, we will get opportunities to be both an example of and a witness in sharing God's love. Try not to miss those opportunities with inaction or silence when those opportunities occur.

REASON #94. We have prayer chains for those in need. A "prayer chain" is dedicated to helping someone or a friend of someone who is ill or needs spiritual support. The person's name is called into the pastor or prayer chain coordinator along with the person's need or request. The coordinator then makes four or five calls to members of the prayer chain, who in turn call four or five other members, thus raising many voices to heaven praying in Jesus's name for the benefit of the subject person of the prayers to add to the person's own supplication for wellness or healing. Many passages in the Bible call on fellow believers to pray. Often those pray statements in the Bible's New Testament are requests for the furtherance of the Gospel and the work of the apostles. We believe God hears all our prayers of praise, petitions for forgiveness, petitions for help, and prayers of thanksgiving. God does his good will for believers without our feeble help or petitions; even still we are told in scripture to "pray without ceasing." When we pray for others, we bring ourselves closer to God through Christ's work, recognizing God's strength and ability to work his will in our world. When we do a prayer chain, our collective prayers recognize that we are all in constant need of all of God's blessings set before us.

REASON #95. Following our faith is not so complicated that one has to live in fear of failure. "You can't do that . . . ," "only if your good enough . . . ," "You must do x, y, z . . . in order to get to heaven," and the list goes on from those radio, TV, and brick-and-mortar preachers who wish to have you live in fear, to look to them instead of looking to God. When they are all asking you to send money to God, but please use their address, consider that a clue that something could be off center in their "Bible-based" message. Lutheran churches, pastors, and outreach efforts stand ready to share the Gospel with you for free. It is OK to be concerned that your faith is not strong enough to be saved; doing so is an assurance that you at least have faith. Praise God for that fountain of doubt of yours, but don't drink from it. Your faith may need a little boost so you feel better about yourself; yet one needs only to look outward to God. His Son, Jesus, is the one doing the heavy lifting for us. It is not complicated; look to the Bible, John 3:16. Jesus's work has the power to absolve our sin, no matter its magnitude in our minds. For the inverse, go to Mark 16:6. For those that reject the Gospel once they have heard, look at Luke 12:47–48. This work of salvation provided for us is not complicated; it never was, never will be, Look at Acts 2:41. Trust the work of Jesus, and not just in your head; keep it in your heart where your emotions reside: Love God. That's all it takes! To find reassurance of that truth, find yourself a seat in the pew at any LCMS church service for a divine service. You will hear we are all sinners; we have fallen short of keeping God's law, but in his love for us he sent Jesus to be our Savior. It's just not that complicated.

REASON #96. We can eat double cheeseburgers on Friday, even during Lent. I remember as a child growing up, many of my running mates who were steeped in religion by their own volition or by demanding parents would lament some of what they had to do or not for religious observance reasons. A popular gripe was having to eat fish on Friday. I, on the other hand, was looking forward to being home and scarfing up as much of my mother's homemade "hamburger pizza" as I could and really never got the connection to why it was good to only eat fish on Friday. These same mates would complain in equal measure about having to "give something up" for Lent. Later I would learn and understand that the giving something up is about remembering Christ's suffering that was his punishment brought about by our sin. As Lutherans we can choose to take on this practice if it helps us feel closer to Jesus and embrace our redemption through his undeserved love for us. There is no requirement to do so. As an adult a way to approach this issue during the time of Lent is to resolve to give up on one of your own well-known and repetitive sins or shortcomings. Pick one and do your best to honor Jesus's suffering by not doing that sin for 40 days. You probably won't make it to 40 days, but if nothing else, you will grow in appreciation for what Jesus's suffering and death and resurrection has accomplished for us.

REASON #97. Heaven would only have one former earth occupant if it took perfection to get there. Maybe three if you wish include the imperfect Enoch and Elijah. Luther's words echo in my ear as I write this section of this book: "grace alone, faith alone, scripture alone." Any religion except occult ones are all about improving your life here on earth and perfecting a life after death into eternity. We do righteous work but are not a work righteous religion. We aspire to be perfect in our daily walk with God but are not. We want to know what God knows but cannot know all. Perfection will never be the human condition when it comes to our bodies, minds, or behaviors; we sin daily; we break the commandments daily. But the Good News we embrace is that we are not doomed by our failure. God inspired men (mankind), the prophets and apostles, to write a book, the Holy Bible, about himself and what he wanted us to know about him as Creator, know about Jesus as Savior, know about the Holy Spirit as our constant companion throughout our lives. Hence Luther's phrase: "scripture alone." Use no other source. Believe, have faith that Jesus died for my sins, yours sins, our (all mankind) sins and won our forgiveness before God through his work of redemption. Hence Luther's phrase: "faith alone." Good works won't work. God did this work, not because of any merit or meritorious work on our part, but because he loves us as a part of his creation. We, those created in the image of God, are the ones he cares about most. His undeserved love for us is that grace. Hence Luther's phrase: "grace alone." A small thimbleful of words succinctly defines access to a universe full of love that brings us the means to be before God and spend eternity with him.

REASON #98. We loathe the idea that every time you sin, it is back to the dunk tank. Some religious Christian faiths practice multiple baptism, others don't recognize infant baptism, and some do a rebaptism if you have committed a grave sin, particularly one where everybody in the congregation knows what you did. Lutherans believe that if you are baptized in the name of the triune God, the water and the Word place an indelible mark on you and your soul as one of God's children, and that only needs doing once. Don't know of any ranchers branding their cattle more than once. Many Bible passages liken God's people, Jesus's followers, to sheep. We are said to be his flock. Even if we are lost and fall away, the ownership mark of our souls does not change; we are his alone. To follow any other practice of multiple baptisms is a mark of denying the power of God's word as truth or puts some human factor into the equation that you must "be of age" to understand or consciously participate in some way. Trust that you don't need to understand God's power; you simply need to accept it. "Thank you, God, for marking me as one of your own!" That's a prayer of thanksgiving for doing that great work for me.

Our one baptism took care of that, obliterating our original sin and marking us as a child of God. We rely on the mercy, grace, and power of God and trust his word that Jesus is Savior and provided our redemption. We are baptized once into the faith to be his. That is all it takes.

As Lutherans we do not limit God's power in any way. The gift of salvation, this gift founded in grace, or his power to affect our lives and assure our salvation is not denied. We count on it and do not look for ways to put man-made limits on God's abilities to do as he wills.

REASON #99. We don't have to knock on doors to tell people about our religion or Jesus or about our salvation through Jesus. We are simply supposed to be (required to be if you like) examples to the community and world at large of what walking in the faith in all areas of our lives looks like. All Christians are called on to be a witness in sharing the Gospel. As Lutherans we can volunteer to do that in a formal, organized way. Doing things like passing out flyers, being part of a traveling choir, and participating in a church-organized outreach event or program are all optional for us. Even doing the knocking on doors to evangelize to others if we choose. We do not require our teens or young adults to do missionary work for a year or two before beginning their adult lives, and yet there are opportunities to do so for those who wish to do it. For the most part we Lutherans are often reluctant to share our faith with strangers, find it challenging to share with friends and acquaintances, and so it's probably good that there is no hard-and-fast requirement for us to be missionaries at home or overseas. Recognizing this shortcoming is the first step to improving our sorry condition. Stepping outside our comfort zone takes an overwhelming reason to change our behavior. And there is only one reason: God loved us enough to bring us into the fold; we should show our love to God and love (care, concern) for our neighbor sufficient to provide a witness of faith in the Gospel message to them in spite of our fear of "personal" rejection. Once shared, the message may stick and work years later. Understand that the rebuffing hearers of the Word are not rejecting us personally; they are rejecting what the Gospel promises to everyone who accepts Jesus and his work of salvation. We can only pray for the hearers, once they have heard it.

REASON #100. We are OK with the dogmatic concept of separation of church and state. As Lutherans we think of whatever government that is in place in our civic life is God's left hand at work. We do not have to like it, but it is necessary for good order. That is a workable, an easy, perspective to take on, as the government is run by elected officials in the United States. Few churches flourish under dictatorships or under single-party-controlled governments or governments that are entirely controlled by religion or atheism. This concept of separation of church and state may well be the invention of the American experiment that has worked for a few hundred years, but the concept may well lead to the downfall of true freedom of religion, that is to say, the free, unencumbered practice of religion.

The concept is embedded in the wording that appears in the First Amendment to the U.S. Constitution: "Congress shall make no law respecting an establishment of religion, or prohibiting the free exercise thereof; or abridging the freedom of speech, or of the press; or the right of the people peaceably to assemble, and to petition the government for a redress of grievances."

In the framers' minds, the first part of the statement about religion prohibited the government from settling on one version of religion to the exclusion of others and prevented the government from taxing the population to support a particular religion or church. The second part of the statement about religion forbade the government from preventing citizens to freely practice any religion. However, our federal government, state governments, and the respective courts have gone too far with this and have condoned a concept that is more freedom "from" any element of religion in the public or civic space rather than freedom "of" practicing any particular religion. There are elements in our society and the world that wish to use the long arm of the government to abolish all religion, and the fight has reached a level of fervor associated more with war rather than discourse.

Quite in spite of the threat posed by the antireligious and the obvious misinterpretation of the First Amendment by the courts, we must still support the principle of keeping the government's hands off religion. The biggest reason is that although our country and its laws are still thought to be based on Judeo-Christian thought and principles, there are other religions (and their principles) we would find quite unacceptable if codified in any way into our existing body of civic law. So even though I personally abhor actions that take Jewish or Christian icons and nativity scenes and so forth out of the public space, protesting this for me would be moving a scintilla in the wrong direction of allowing government to be favoring a religion I would not like. One could say that removing these religious elements and icons by the hand of the government favors an "antireligion religion," and those that think that would be right; it does.

REASON #101. There is no need to fear the end of our life. Lutherans trust the Gospel message such that crossing through the curtain of death brings us to the place where God, Jesus, and the

Holy Spirit abide in all their fullness. We believe we will join the throngs of Jewish and Christian faithful who have gone before us to join the chorus to be with and praise God through all eternity. Sure, the prospect of dying is gloomy; earth after all, God's whole created universe, is a pretty good place to be most any day. Heaven is better; the hope of things to come should sustain us through those trying times here on earth. This was exemplified for me when my Aunt Anita was facing serious heart surgery that would give her a few more years if successful. A friend of hers a few days before the surgery asked her, "What will happen if you die?" Her instant reply, "My friends will miss me." This example of hers is a clear message that she accepted her earthly mortality and trusted in the Gospel.

Although some, when loved ones leave us, say things like "He (or she) is one of God's angels now," that is not what the Bible teaches us. God has all the heavenly angels he needs. We can act like angels on earth, that is to say, do good works out of love for what God has done for us, but doing good works does not make us into angels when we die either. If you have said this in the past to comfort people when they have lost someone, please stop doing this. Instead remind them of the promises of the Gospel message and the reunion of all saints in heaven. Good angels are those that follow the wisdom and direction of God, and those that do not follow are not good angels. Good angels are God's messengers to us. There is much to learn about God's angels in the Bible, but when we live and die in the faith, we are saints, not angels; saints in daily life and in death. It is my understanding that any saint, a famous one or you or me, is ranked above the angels. This being true, wanting to condemn a loved one or a child who has died all too young from cancer to angel status in heaven does the person no favors and confuses the bereaved about their own earthly and heavenly relationship to God in heaven and the reuniting of saints in heaven when they too pass on.

REASON #102 (BONUS). It is OK to never fully understand the mysteries surrounding the triune God we worship. Some things just need to be accepted as the mysteries they are to us mere mortals on this earth. This is a tough topic for new converts to the Christian faith. We say we worship one God in three Persons. To our human thinking, this makes no sense. In the Athanasian Creed we say one "substance" in referring to God and Jesus (his Son).

A key point in Christianity is that God comes to us; we don't have to work to earn our way to him. In the Old Testament there are only a handful of theophany events where God was manifest to man; Adam and Eve and Moses are examples. In the New Testament Jesus stayed long enough not only to do his saving work but also to teach his disciples the relationship between us mortals and God.

It should not be hard to think that from all these examples in Holy Scripture that this is the same "entity," the same "purpose," that is at work in the world from the Old and New Testament record.

It is OK to not fully understand the concept of the triune God; it is not OK, however, to not accept the Trinity, It is one of the many things you will learn more about when your "entity," your soul, crosses through to the other side of the curtain of death.

So, to understand this fully, know that we are all sinners and in need of forgiveness. Luther is quoted to have said "Sin boldly" because we can trust that Jesus's sacrifice covers our sins: past, present, and future. There is no point making up new or imaginary sins to further burden our Lord and Savior.

The Lutheran Narrative

Some, such as my wife, have called us Lutherans or being Lutheran as being "Catholic without the guilt." Others have called us "run-away Catholics." There's some truth in both of those phrases, so let me explain how I think about our history as a Lutheran Christian belief system. To my thinking there are four time periods of significance in the Christian faith. The first time period started with Jesus's death and resurrection. During these first three to five years, the church and beliefs surrounding Jesus could very well have easily died out. Nearly everything in government and culture was working against the faith's survival. Yet through God's will and grace, the beliefs survived against all the odds. During these first few years, there were no denominations as we know them today. There were those citizens of many nearby nations adhering to the faith and belief system, and others that were "Christian" in name only. The next period occurred, say, five years after Christ's death on the cross and resurrection to about AD 400. During this second time period, the church grew and became more organized, more accepted, and its identity and self-identity became more refined and recorded. At this point it was still only mostly one belief system with few significant divisions in beliefs. The teachings of Jesus and his apostles were shared and became more understood by those living in the faith. It was during this second time period, in every way, the Christian church shared universally in values and beliefs. You can read about its progress and trials and tribulations in early nonbiblical historical works such as the "Confession of Justin" and others. The third time period was from about AD 400 to October, 31, 1517. During this period, there were splinter priests and clusters of believers that broke away from the teaching of the catholic (meaning universal) church, even as early as 1050 and 1100. By the time Luther came on the scene, for the most part the Roman Catholic Church was firmly rooted and operated in the known Western world of the time as the only Christian church body, with its hierarchy and organization that had begun to evolve with many man-made rules, beliefs, and traditions brought about by councils and popes during this third-phase early period. Luther hanging up his points for debate set loose what is nothing short of a revolution that leads to rebranding and picking up on nuances from the Bible and expanding them to divisions of the church in ways he would have not ever imagined, intended, or wanted. We are still living in that time period. The problem is that this branding and rebranding of the message is taking away from the core messages of early Christianity and often diluting the central message of the Gospel. The reality is that they, meaning all the denominations afoot today, can't all be right; can't all be teaching the true doctrine as God intended it to be taught.

Here is an example. There really is not going to be a thousand-year reign of the Retuned Christ on an earthly Kingdom. And no matter how special you are or how strongly you believe it, you are not going to be raptured to heaven like Elijah from the Old Testament. You are going to have to die first to find fellowship in heaven like every one of the saints before you. No matter how many good works you do, you are not going to buy your way into heaven, one of Luther's key points. If I am a good person, God is going to permit me to go to heaven even if I am not religious. Sorry if this offends you, but if you have these mistaken beliefs and many other ideas that reduce or deny the Gospel, beliefs that could literally fill books and do, you just happen to be wrong. This is one of the very big things I savor about being a member of the Lutheran Church–Missouri Synod. LCMS adheres closest to the teachings of Martin Luther, who in turn returned the "church" closer to the unadulterated teaching of the Holy Scriptures and the church's early roots and core beliefs systems in place during the first 400 years after Christ's death and resurrection. What Luther left behind and abandoned were the silly man-made traditions and rules that serve only to keep you from understanding the true message of what Christ's saving work accomplished for us. Luther, a 34-year-old rebel, who had no intention of being one. Luther's education that included two bachelor's degrees and a doctor's degree contributed to his ability to reason out the 95 theses that began the Reformation. There were two things Luther had a handle on: logical thinking and critical thinking, using them to test every and any point of view put before him. This talent of critical thinking while trusting God and the Holy Scriptures for the answers, and not the tradition and institutions, is what brought about the Reformation.

How I Came to Write This Book

My father's family was Methodist, as many of those from Cornwall, England, were. I do believe my father went to the Lutheran Church at times, but his solid early exposure to Methodism I think made him a little more inclined on a Sunday morning to take the double-barrel 12 gauge for a walk down the railroad tracks with old Shep, a collie mix, to see if a rabbit or two or three might find their way into one of our stewpots. In spite of that, he must have been a visitor to our Lutheran Church, as our Lutheran pastor conducted my and my sibling' baptisms and confirmation services. I am fairly certain that if my father did not believe he would be counted as saved by Jesus's blood on the cross, he would have found the lure of the weekly church service a little more powerful than a walk through the woods. My father died when I was only two years old, so my memory only covers a few events dating back that far. I remember his funeral day and the night before he died. Both those times were vividly burned into my then two-year-old memory and still are with me. He was born in 1903 in Calumet, Michigan, and died in Laurium, Michigan, in 1951. My sister claims his funeral service was conducted from the Methodist Church in Laurium. A lot of folks in the town liked my father, and over 500 people showed up to sign the guest book at his visitation and funeral. To me, that shouts out volumes about the kind of life he led and the kind of person he was. Seriously, the only people that really need to be at a Christian funeral are the dearly departed, the undertaker that delivers the body in the casket to the gravesite, the preacher who reads a bit of scripture and leads a prayer or two over the open ground, the guy who shovels the dirt back in the hole, and the bereaved if there are any. My father obviously had a lot of friends, and many would miss him, but no one person more than my mother, who lived another 55 years to 2006 and never remarried. She was 96 when she passed over to the other side of the curtain of death to be counted as another one of those saints thankful to Jesus and forever praising God there.

The night before my father's imminent death, I was brought into his bed to let him say goodbye to me. He told my mother, "Keep an eye on this one; he is going to be different." I remember hearing his labored breathing and what I would later learn as a sound that some nurses call the death rattle. About a week later I remember seriously disturbing the peace in our neighborhood with my crying and carrying on in the dining room of our house when every one of my older brothers and my sister went to the funeral to say goodbye to my Dad, Leslie (NMN) Brewer, and I was not allowed to go. This briefly accounts for my father's Lutheran ties, which it is fair to call loose ties, but ties nonetheless.

The more interesting clan story is how my mother's family—she and her sisters, one brother, and her mother and father—became Missouri Synod Lutherans, and maybe both of her grandmothers too although I am not sure about them. My grandfather, on my mother's side of the family, was a building contractor and at some time was the mayor of the Village of Laurium. They were not rich, but they did quite OK financially for the time. Had cars early on; my grandmother had a driver's license, which was rare for a woman, and drove Henry's latest Ford wherever she needed to go. As fate would have it, they lived in the middle of the block between the Finnish language Apostolic Lutheran Church of which they were members in good standing and the Missouri Synod German and English Language Lutheran Church founded by, no surprise, early German immigrants to the area. On Sunday after church one week, my grandfather invited the Apostolic church pastor and his family over for Sunday dinner, which may have been a fairly common thing to do then. The short version of this story is that they came back nearly every Sunday, and the pastor's family brought more family members with them, and finally they began to invite friends of the Apostolic church pastor to Sunday dinner at my grandparents' house so close to the church. My grandfather, Oscar, also known as John, maybe did not mind so much, but he was not the one cooking or cleaning up for two dozen people every Sunday afternoon. So the story goes that on one Sunday morning my grandmother said to my grandfather: "Put the kids in the car and take them down to the other end of the block to the German Lutheran Church. Their Sunday school starts in 20 minutes. We are not going to 'that' church today." Well my mother and aunts and uncle kept going to the German Lutheran Church, and pretty soon my grandparents followed. So that is how it happened in a nutshell. I guess it is a good thing the kids did not get turned away for not being German. So was it divine intervention, or am I just plain Lucky to Be Lutheran? Decide for yourself.

Accordingly, I want to be clear here: I hold no negative feelings for the Apostolic Lutheran Church, its members, or my grade school and high school friends who attended this particular church denomination. After all, I was almost one of them. They too are God-fearing people rooted in faith in every way. I am thankful though that I was instead indoctrinated into a Lutheran denomination that takes the scholarly study of the Bible very seriously and insists on a higher level of biblical education for its pastors, deacons and deaconesses, and parochial school teachers. Equally importantly thankful for a church that historically and contemporarily holds high and adheres to the foundational principles of Christian teaching and Lutheran tradition found in the scriptures and the Book of Concord.

I have one other vivid, very early childhood memory from the time before I was two years old, although many might dispute this by saying it is impossible to harbor a memory that old. For the skeptics, I have talked to at least one other person who has a very early memory, in this case actually remembering being born. My very early childhood memory is not my birth; it is my baptism. I was there, awake, and I remember, not the words, not the water so much, but that I was there in the church as an infant: I can see the pastor's face, my parents and sponsors, the cross, the candles, the ornate altar, can hear the music, see the white I was wearing, all in my very oldest memory. I was very much present and aware something was happening as I became God's child, present for the one event that would begin to shape me for the rest of my earthly life—and as Lutherans say, prepared me for the life of the world to come.

About the Author

Dennis was baptized Dennis Carl Brewer into the faith in the Lutheran Church–Missouri Synod, Wisconsin District, at St. Paul Lutheran Church on Tamarack Street in the little Village of Laurium, Michigan, in the month of September of 1949. As of this writing, the church still stands today as it serves the people of the Copper Country. Dennis began attending Sunday school and church services at a very early age. His mother, Verna, was a Sunday school teacher, pianist, and organist for the Sunday school and pinch hitter on the church's pipe organ for Sunday services. His mom also sang in the church's choir. As a teenager, he was confirmed in this same church and later taught Sunday school for a while when he was still in his teens. Dennis attended and was a member of the now nonoperational Walther League during his high school years. As a lifelong Lutheran adult, Mr. Brewer served as a deacon, trustee, and office holder in various Lutheran churches and once was a congregational president. Mostly he savored being less involved and felt more rewarded for just warming the wood, sitting in a pew on Sunday mornings and trying his best to stay awake for the whole sermon and to pay attention to that sought-after message of salvation for all and its reassurance for life. Knowing full well he needed to hear it more than anyone else present.

However, always a Christian and lifelong believer in the fact that God was the one doing the saving work through Christ, Dennis did not always live a "goody two shoes" life sheltered in the shadow of the church steeple or hiding from real life in the church basement. He lived his life in the world and was not always of the world, yet at many junctures succumbed to regretful sin many times, as many other, perhaps all, believers do.

His parallel secular life included careers in the U.S. Navy starting in 1967 and rising to the rank of Chief Petty Officer prior to his twenty-fourth birthday. Navy time included training duty on the Great Lakes and on the East Coast and sea duty on a repair ship that took visits to foreign countries in the Western Pacific, and he served on shore duty as a recruiter for six years. While serving on board the USS Prairie (AD-15) on WestPac cruises, he participated in the chaplain's projects with his shipmates and helped indigenous people in the Philippines and Taiwan. After serving in the Navy, he attended college as an Army R.O.T.C. cadet and achieved his goal of earning a bachelor of science degree in business administration from Michigan Technological University and a commission as a Second Lieutenant in the U.S. Army Reserve. After graduating from the U.S. Army Engineer Officer Basic Course at Fort Belvoir, Virginia, he transferred his commission to the Michigan Military Establishment and served for over 12 years in various engineer units of the Michigan Army National Guard and the State Area Command Headquarters before accepting retirement in 1993 as a Captain Engineer Officer. The civic concept of being a citizen soldier and wanting to give back to his state and nation was still ingrained, leading to his staying in government service where he worked for the Michigan Department of Military Affairs, Department of Management and Budget, and Department of Information Technology, before retiring again in 2006. Beginning in 2008 he and his wife, Penny R. Peterson, invested the next eight years getting to know a bit more about their native land and fellow citizens by full-timing in their Fleetwood Terra 36T LX motor home, visiting 43 states before finding a landing zone in the desert of Arizona near Tucson, where Dennis found employment with the State of Arizona Air National Guard. During this travel time, they also often worked as work campers, sharing and giving back a little at places where they could be useful and add some value to someone else's life.